Fenian Diary

DR C.W. SULLIVAN III is Professor of English at East Carolina University and a member of the Welsh Academy. He is the author of *Welsh Celtic Myth in Modern Fantasy* (1989); editor of *The Mabinogi: A Book of Essays* (1996), *Young Adult Science Fiction* (1999), *The Dark Fantastic: Selected Essays from the Ninth International Conference on the Fantastic in the Arts* (1997), *Science Fiction for Young Readers* (1993), and *As Tomorrow Becomes Today* (1974); and a co-editor of *Worldviews and the American West: The Life of the Place Itself* (2000) and *Herbal and Magical Medicine: Traditional Healing Today* (1992). He is the Immediate Past President of the International Association for the Fantastic in the Arts, the editor of *The Children's Folklore Review,* a co-editor of *Celtic Cultural Studies,* and a member of the editorial board for *Para*doxa: Studies in World Literary Genres.* His articles on mythology, folklore, fantasy, and science fiction have appeared in a variety of anthologies and journals.

Convict Ship "Hougoumont"
(At Sea near mouth of English Channel)
15th October 1867.

"The Wanderer far from those he loves, and all his heart holds dear,
Oft pauses as he onward roams, to check the rising tear,
When thoughts of home and by-gone days come crowding o'er his brain
How sweet the voice within that says hope on we'll meet again,"

On Tuesday the 24th September, whilst very busily employed at
(to me) very disagreeable occupation of picking "Oakum," I heard steps
approach along the corridor and hall opposite my cell door: instantly
the iron gate and massive wooden door of my cell were flung open, and
the order "Stand at ye gate" given. I, glad of anything that would even
for a moment twart the monotony, or break the wretched grave-like
silence of the place, immediately came to "attention" at the door; and found
my visitors to be the Head Warder Harvey and some Warders of lower grade.
Then for the first time I learned that I was to be sent to Australia.
I received the news with a very bad grace, and protested in the
strongest terms against being sent,—but recollecting that I had no
voice in the matter, and that God should, I strove to make the most
of it, and drown the bitter feelings which filled my breast, by
fiercely working at, or rather tearing the tough coir,— I really
felt wretched,— the thought of being sent 14,000 miles away from
my dear wife and children,— from all that I love on earth; with the
fact staring me in the face that I should not again for years see
them, caused me to feel an acute agony that I never before felt;
and plunged my whole being into the deepest melancholy.—
Imagination was to conjure up before me, the tearful eyes & sorrowful
face of my dear Kate,—gazing at our dear children, who want her to
tell them "why their Pa does not come home"—whilst she picturing to
herself the terrible distance which divides us, in her bitter sorrow reasons
back the answer she would not (even to herself) dare to speak, fearing
to look the dread reality in the face.— On this the most trying
hour of my life; when all other resources failed, I prostrate myself
before my Maker, and in prayer found a soothing relief; the softening
influence of which calmed my thoughts, and caused me to look
with altered feelings, one a more hopeful eye on the hour so much
dreaded future.— On the evening of this day I was allowed to write
home, and I fear if I penned my letter in accordance with the
tenor of my feelings, it was a very melancholy epistle, and not
in the style which I should have written.— however I now hope

Fenian Diary

Denis B. Cashman
on board the Hougoumont

with additional poems by Cashman,
John Boyle O'Reilly, John Flood, and others

Edited and Introduced by
Dr C.W. Sullivan III

WOLFHOUND PRESS

First published in 2001 by
Wolfhound Press Ltd
68 Mountjoy Square
Dublin 1, Ireland
Tel: (353-1) 874 0354
Fax: (353-1) 872 0207

British Library Cataloguing in Publication Data
A catalogue record for this book is available from the British Library.

ISBN 0-86327-858-2

10 9 8 7 6 5 4 3 2 1

Front Cover Photo of Denis B. Cashman, courtesy Kevin Cusack
Frontispiece: First page of Denis B. Cashman's diary, courtesy East Carolina University Manuscript Archives)
Illustrations: Tana French
Cover Design: Wolfhound Press
Typeset in Calisto and Splendid by Wolfhound Press
Printed in the UK by Cox & Wyman Ltd., Reading, Berks.

For Ann

Contents

Preface

Setting the Record Straight

In 1982, a local resident, Dr Alfred Sheehy of Belhaven, North Carolina, donated fourteen items to the East Carolina University Manuscript Archives. The archive records describe the materials as follows: papers (1865–1887), including a diary, correspondence, [newspaper] clippings, a book of poetry, a biography, a photograph, and an announcement. The announcement is for a twenty-fifth wedding anniversary party, the biography is a first edition of Denis B. Cashman's *Life of Michael Davitt*, and the diary is the original diary kept by Denis B. Cashman aboard the *Hougoumont* during his transportation to Australia, 1867–1868.

As I was working on other projects at the time and then went into an administrative post, I had little time to investigate this intriguing collection. But in 1995, after stepping back into a professorial position, I checked out the materials and decided to work with them. After several trips to Boston, a preliminary trip to Ireland in 1996, and a spring leave in Ireland in 1998, I have become excited by these materials and by the opportunity to publish the diary.

Other scholars who have published on the Fenians, and especially on the Fenians transported to Australia, have used quotations from Cashman and referred to the diary, but they have not been using the original source. They have quoted from excerpts published in the journal *Ave Maria* (June 1950) or from copies in the Battye and the Mitchell libraries in Australia. While these sources are, for the most part, sound, they do have some faults. The materials in *Ave Maria* are far from complete, and there are some inaccuracies in the copies that exist in the Battye and Mitchell collections.

Although there is still much to be learned about the life of Denis B. Cashman, I believe that the publication of his diary will provide scholars with a complete and accurate text carefully transcribed from the original. Much of what we do know of Cashman's life is included in the introduction to this book; I hope to continue researching to find out more about this very interesting man, who was a friend and companion to such more famous Irishmen as John Boyle O'Reilly, Michael Davitt, James Stephens, John Devoy, and others.

The Diary

The diary itself is a part of collection number 458.1 in the East Carolina University Manuscript Archives, and it rests in a cardboard envelope inside the larger carton that houses all of the Cashman materials.

The diary is currently bound in a patterned, dark-brown leather or leatherette cover, 4¾ by 7¼ inches, which is clearly newer than the diary itself. Inside that cover is a 4¾ by 7³/₈ parchment cover, without decoration, into which the diary is stitched. At one time, the parchment may have been glued to the leatherette. The parchment appears to have been some of the official stock from the firm of Dobbyn & Tandy, where Cashman worked as a law clerk, as the name 'Waterford' appears on it, along with amounts of money and names of officials of the city and the church; it is obviously not a full sheet from a copybook, and may have been cut from a larger sheet which had been discarded for some reason.

The individual pages of the diary, many of which have pulled away from the stitching, are 4¾ by 7½ inches. The paper is light and thin, and Cashman's handwriting is small, crowded, and neat — often so filling the page that subsequent wear or damage has erased some of the letters and, here and there, a word or two. The diary is fifty-eight pages long, including a selection of poems that appeared in *The Wild Goose* and several others as well. A Thomas McCarthy Fennell poem, which is at the front of the diary, is on one side of a single sheet of paper and was written for Cashman; it may have been slipped into the diary as a single sheet rather than written onto one of the existing diary pages.

In the box housing the collection, there is also a pouch with a snap-close cover, into which the diary would fit. It appears to be genuine leather but is probably not as old as the diary.

Editing and Introducing the Diary

First of all, let me say that the text of Denis B. Cashman's diary that follows in these pages is as accurate as is possible. The diary itself is almost a hundred and fifty years old now and, although it has been handled well over the years, there are places where the writing is barely legible at best and quite confusing at worst. In addition, such small marks as full stops, commas, quotation marks, and apostrophes are often faded and sometimes obscured by creases or folds in the paper. Given these limitations, and the need to continue handling the diary very carefully, I have used everything from hand-held magnifying glasses to enlarged photocopies in an attempt to read the difficult parts; in most cases, I believe that I have succeeded.

Second, while the Cashman diary is quite clear as it stands and interesting in its own right, I have provided an introduction that covers the main events of Cashman's life — in Ireland, Australia, and the United States. His continuing support of Fenian causes after he was pardoned, especially the *Catalpa* mission, belies his pre-trial statement that he was remorseful and would have resigned from the Fenians had they not threatened his life and the lives of his family. And much of the rest of his biography both sheds light on what he wrote in the diary and is, in turn, illuminated by the diary.

Third, I have looked at the diary from a rhetorical perspective. The inspiration for this approach came from Andrew Hassam's *Sailing to Australia* (1994), a rhetorical examination of emigrant diaries. My argument here — still in its initial stages — is that the convict diary, precisely because it *is* a convict diary, will have a significantly different rhetorical structure from the emigrant diary. This is an area in which I would like to do more work.

Fourth, although I have made some comments about the Fenians, I have not provided a full account of the history of the Fenian movement. That history has been most ably presented by others, most recently Thomas Keneally in *The Great Shame* (1998). I believe that many readers will already know that history, and that those who do not will certainly seek out the experts listed in the bibliography.

Fifth, I have left inconsistencies in dating, spelling, use of punctuation marks, capitalisation and word forms (Cashman uses both 'Albatross's' and 'Albatrosses' for the plural of the word — and he almost always puts the word in quotation marks), so that the reader can better appreciate how Cashman accomplished the physical act of writing aboard the often-pitching ship and also appreciate what a good prose stylist he was — even in those circumstances. It is also interesting to note that Cashman and his fellow transportees generally used 'American' spellings rather than UK/Irish spellings — 'color' for 'colour', 'fraternized' for 'fraternised', 'practice' for 'practise', and the like. Occasionally, however, there is a UK/Irish spelling. I have left them all as I found them.

Sixth, I have integrated the poetry that was published in *The Wild Goose*, a newspaper written aboard the *Hougoumont*, into the diary at the appropriate dates. I believe that placing the poems there helps to complete the picture the diary is presenting. Additional poems by Denis B. Cashman, John Boyle O'Reilly and John Flood, and other poems that pertain to the Fenians' transportation to Australia, follow the conclusion of the diary.

Finally, let me say that this work, which began as an interesting pursuit, has become an important endeavour for me. I have found Cashman's narrative compelling, as much for what he seems to be saying (and feeling) between the lines as for the actual day-to-day account of the four-month voyage to Australia. From the diary and the relatively few things we now know about his life, he must have been quite a fascinating man. I hope to get to know him better through future research.

Acknowledgements

This book has come to publication through the efforts of a great many people and institutions.

The Irish American Cultural Institute, administering funds from the O'Shaughnessy Family, the British Embassy in Washington, DC, and East Carolina University, provided major grants for travel to Ireland and Northern Ireland in 1996 and 1998; and the College of Arts and Sciences at East Carolina University awarded me a semester's research leave in the spring of 1998.

Individual scholars who helped along the way include Thomas O'Connor, Boston College; Father Peter Conley, editor, *The Pilot*; George Ryan, reporter (retired), *The Pilot*; Ruth Ann Harris, Northeastern University; Karen Ogden,

Harvard University; M. Kevin Cusack (editor of the John Sarsfield Casey diary), Paget, Bermuda; Walter McGrath, Cork; Tim Cadigan, Cork County Library; Trevor Parkhill, Ulster Museum, Belfast; Patrick Fitzgerald, Ulster-American Folk Park, Omagh; Tom Quinlan, National Archives, Dublin; David Fitzpatrick, University of Dublin; Patrick McCarthy, Dublin; Dermot Power, Waterford Municipal Library; Andy Bennett, Navan Library, Navan; Leigh Hays, J.S. Battye Library of West Australian History; Brendan Woods and Dermot McGuckin, Perth, Australia; and Alison Kibler, Downer, Australia.

At East Carolina University, Dr Bruce Southard, English Department Chair, Dr W. Keats Sparrow, Dean of the College of Arts and Science, and Dr Tom Feldbush, Vice Chancellor for Research, were extremely supportive of this project. Ms Pat Guyette, of the university's Inter-Library Loan Service, was especially helpful in obtaining various items I needed to see. Ms Kathryn Fladenmuller, my 1997–1998 graduate assistant, and Ms Amanda Bryant Brooks, then a secretary in the department, deserve thanks for taking care of day-to-day business and helping me keep in touch with other scholars in the field while I was in Ireland in the spring of 1998. I would also like to thank Ms Laurie Evans; without her generosity and computer skills, I might still be trying to prepare this manuscript for publication.

Three people deserve special acknowledgements. Don Lennon, Curator of the East Carolina University Manuscript Collection, in which the Cashman diary resides, and his staff were both encouraging and helpful while I was working with the diary itself. Seamus Cashman, Wolfhound Press, Dublin, not only agreed to publish these materials but offered sound editing advice. First and last, of course, Ann Sullivan, my wife, gave me continued support and, with minimal protest, allowed me to go off and spend much of the spring of 1998 researching in Northern Ireland and Ireland.

The publishers wish to acknowledge East Carolina University who provided a subvention towards the publication of this book.

Introduction
Cashman and the Diary

Denis B. Cashman: Irishman, American, Fenian[1]

Rebel in Ireland

In the fall of 1867, the *Hougoumont* sailed from England with sixty-two or sixty-three (Amos 87 and Evans 57; Keneally 482) Fenian prisoners, some of the total 280 male convicts being transported to Australia. The *Hougoumont* was a four-masted Blackwall frigate about 167 feet long and 34 feet wide, and she weighed 875 tons. Launched at Moulmein, Burma, in 1852 and originally one of Duncan Dunbar's fleet, she was named for the Hougoumont Farm, a site at the battle of Waterloo; when she became a transport ship carrying emigrants and then convicts to Australia, she was owned by Luscombe of London and on charter to the British government (Bateson 283; Evans 55). She was the last official convict ship to Australia, and one of the young Fenians aboard her was Denis B. Cashman, late of Waterford, convicted of felony treason and sentenced to seven years' penal servitude.

Denis B. Cashman, born in 1842 in Dungarvan, Co. Waterford, was a native of Waterford in the Province of Munster but was living in Dublin at the time of his arrest. In 1858, during the initial stages of its formation, Cashman had joined the Irish Republican Brotherhood, the Fenians; he would have been about sixteen at the time. One of his first major contributions to the movement may have been to help hide Lawrence O'Brien in his own home in the late 1850s. O'Brien had escaped from a British prison in Ireland and was preparing to flee to America. Some thirty years later, in Boston, O'Brien and Cashman would be two of the pallbearers for the body of John Boyle O'Reilly.

Cashman was married in 1862. Over the next few years he worked as a law clerk for the firm of Dobbyn & Tandy in Waterford,[2] and he and his wife Catherine became the parents of three boys. He must have also worked tirelessly for the Fenian movement, because between the late 1850s and his arrest in 1867 he rose in the ranks to become the Centre of the Waterford Circle. This meant that he had the power to enlist and swear in new members, but it was also a very dangerous position: an informer or informers were pointing out the Waterford leaders to the police, who then arrested them. By 1864 or 1865, these Fenian activities brought Cashman to Dublin, where he got to know his immediate superior in the organisation, Dr Edward Power, as well as James Stephens and other leaders of the organisation. In fact, it may have been Stephens himself who asked Cashman to come to Dublin.

According to official records, Cashman lived at 5 Preston Street in Dublin and was reported to have engaged in 'manufacturing rifle cartridges' (*Ireland: Irish Crimes Records*, 1866, 155a); he was also reported to have 'accompanied [Dr Edward] Power in distributing rifles' ('12 January 1867', *Fenian Police Reports*, 1864–1883). On the basis of that 'evidence', he was arrested under the Habeas Corpus Suspension Act on 12 January 1867. The arrest warrant describes him as an 'intelligent young man of considerable influence' (*Ireland: Irish Crimes Records*, 1862 to 1865, 104). In a pre-trial interview which took place in the infamous Kilmainham Gaol, Cashman soon 'acknowledged that he was at one time a Member of the Fenian consp[irac]y. But when he became aware of its objects [*sic*] he gave up all connection with it & sought to induce others to abandon their evil intentions' (*Ireland: Irish Crimes Records*, 1866, 155a). Cashman further explained that 'Having got himself entangled in the meshes of Fenianism, considerations for his personal safety prevented him from even attempting his extrication ... until the strong arm of the law accomplished it for him, and found for him a Sanctuary within the prison walls' (Superintendent Daniel Ryan np).

On 19 February 1867, Cashman was brought to trial, where he pled guilty, was convicted, and was sentenced to seven years' penal servitude for felony treason (*Ireland: Irish Crimes Records*, 1866, 155a). According to an obituary that appeared in *The Pilot*, 16 January 1897, the prosecuting attorney told Cashman that, in view of his youth, he could plead guilty to a minor offence. '"No," replied Cashman, "if I had my life to live over I would do it again. I am willing to die for Ireland"' (5ff). Superintendent Ryan, recalling his interview with Cashman in Kilmainham Gaol, noted that, while Cashman swore he had wanted to leave the Fenian movement, he also said that 'not for the value in gold of the British empire would he become an informer' (np).

Cashman's arrest was part of a major movement by the British government to counter the threat that the Fenians posed in Ireland. By 1864, according to some accounts, there was a solid civilian and military organisation ready to strike a major blow for Irish independence. James Stephens claimed to have eighty thousand sworn civilian members and another fifteen thousand in the military, although other sources believe the total number, including both civilian and military, to have been closer to fifty-five thousand (Newsinger 40). With those numbers, and expecting substantial support from America, especially in the form of trained military officers fresh from the Civil War, Stephens and the other leaders planned an uprising before the end of 1865. Unfortunately for the Fenian cause, the order was not given; and the British, in the meantime, had finally gathered enough evidence, from informers as well as from their own investigations, to strike first. Police raids began on 14 September 1865; Stephens himself was arrested on 11 November (though he escaped less than two weeks later); the Habeas Corpus Act was suspended in February of 1866, and mass arrests began all over Ireland. By March of 1867, when the Fenians finally made their move, 'the movement had been seriously weakened by arrests, its organization inside the British army had been neutralised and the American wing had dissipated its resources' in an unsuccessful attack on Canada[3] (Newsinger 58–59).

On 13 July 1867, Catherine Cashman wrote to the Lord Lieutenant General and General Governor of Ireland on behalf of her husband, asking for clemency. She reminded the Lord Lieutenant General that Dobbyn & Tandy had sent a letter of support, and explained that her husband's salary was necessary for her support and the support of their three children (especially as she had, since his arrest, 'pledged or pawned her small stock of clothing to feed her infant children'). She not only asserted that her husband 'had learned a lesson that will insure his being truly penitent for the past and as a Loyal Subject for the future', but also supported his contention that he had wanted to leave the movement: 'the prisoner both preceding his arrest and subsequently previous to his trial has again and again stated to your memorialist the folly that he was guilty of and how duped and misled and his determination to give up all connection with the matter so soon as he safely could without danger to his life' (Catherine Cashman np).

This kind of defence seems to have been common among the Fenians, but in Cashman's case, it may almost have worked. In his report of 31 July 1867, Superintendent Daniel Ryan both supported the truth of Catherine Cashman's statement and spoke on behalf of the prisoner:

> The prisoner is a man differing in many ways from the generality of those apprehended for Fenianism. He is evidently a man of respectable parents, and one whose education was attended to. He filled respectable situations in both Waterford & Dublin, and in the latter city he was clerk to Wm Smyth, law agent for the Corporation, who held him in the highest estimation and would have gone to any amount of security for him at the time of his apprehension, incredulous that one of such excellent character, as was Cashman, could have any connection with the Conspiracy. (np)

Ryan closed the letter by saying that 'if it would not be inconsistent with sound policy, and not the establishing of an awkward and embarrassing precedent, it would be a positive Charity to this man and his tender family to mitigate, in some measure, the punishment inflicted on him' (np). By this time, however, Denis B. Cashman was in solitary confinement in Millbank Prison in England and would soon be on his way to Australia.

Prisoner Aboard the Hougoumont

The first Irish convicts to arrive in Australia were transported there aboard a fleet of ships that arrived in Sydney Harbour in January of 1788, exactly eighty years before the last convict ship, the *Hougoumont*, would bring Cashman and his fellow prisoners to Fremantle, on the opposite side of the continent. Transportation ceased with the *Hougoumont* primarily because there were enough free immigrants in Australia (along with descendants of the first convicts to be sent there) to object to the British government's continuing use of Australia as a dumping ground for its criminals.

In his novel, *Moondyne*, based on his experiences in Australia, John Boyle O'Reilly wrote an account of the conditions aboard a convict ship:

> Only those who have stood within the bars, and heard the din of devils and the appalling sounds of despair, blended in a diapason that made every hatch-mouth a vent of hell, can imagine the horrors of the hold of a convict ship. (214)

In his obituary for J.B. O'Reilly, Cashman presented a similar description of the conditions on that voyage:

> A three month's voyage on board a British convict ship to an Irish political prisoner is an indescribable horror. It is utterly monotonous, and is only varied occasionally by hearing the cat on a convict's back, the funeral services now and again, followed with a splash and the fins of a shark or two darting after the prize; the constant rattling of chains on limbs and hands of the unfortunate convicts. (qtd. in Amos 101)

While these statements have a certain basis in truth, they are much more descriptive of the fate of the 'common criminals' than of the situation for the Fenian transportees.

Cashman's diary presents a somewhat different picture of life aboard the *Hougoumont*. The Fenians themselves sought to counter the monotony that Cashman mentions by holding singing and storytelling sessions in the evenings. These were immediately successful and grew in popularity and participation, even drawing in the initially reluctant O'Reilly, as the voyage progressed. In his diary, Thomas McCarthy Fennell contrasts the Fenians' entertainment with that of the other prisoners — who, he recounts, spent their time telling stories of their previous crimes or planning new crimes for Australia (Fennell 77–79).

In addition to the evenings' entertainments — and with the assistance of Father Delany, who provided the materials — several of the Fenians, including Cashman, created a newspaper, *The Wild Goose*, which appeared seven times during the voyage. Cashman drew the ornamental headings, which were entwined with shamrocks, wrote the sub-headings, and contributed occasionally to the contents — only one of the twenty-five poems to appear in *The Wild Goose* was by Cashman. But most of all, as Cashman (just out of solitary confinement) reports, they talked with one another and provided a friendship which eased the pain of being separated from loved ones and homeland.

Most interesting, perhaps, is that the civilian Fenians, and later O'Reilly and perhaps some of the other military Fenians, were separated from the rest of the convicts. As Cashman notes several times in the diary, the Fenians felt that they had little in common with the other convicts. This attitude seems not unfounded, for, as the evening entertainments and the poems and essays in *The Wild Goose* indicate, many of the Fenians were educated and literate men; in fact, several, including John Flood, O'Reilly, and Cashman, went on to careers in journalism after attaining their freedom.[4] The Fenians were allowed the freedom to walk the deck of the ship and were fed reasonably well, given a ration of wine every day, and provided with tobacco. Moreover, the deaths and punishments to which O'Reilly and Cashman refer were primarily among the other convicts, as the Fenians were extremely well-behaved aboard ship and only incurred punishment for occasional minor infractions (Amos 148). This is not to say that the Fenians enjoyed a pleasure cruise, but it is clear from their own accounts and the reports from the ship's officers that their situation was not, at least physically, a 'hellish' one.

But even Cashman's diary probably does not give the complete picture, as he and the others who were keeping records were instructed to avoid any 'political' writing. O'Reilly's plans for seizing the ship and sailing it to America, for example, are hinted at in Cashman's writings but became a matter of record only after O'Reilly and Cashman were safely in America (Evans 64). On a personal level, however, Cashman's diary does record the changing attitude of a man who begins the voyage in despair of ever seeing his wife and homeland again, but slowly comes to see his probable future in Australia in a positive light, imagining himself a free man there and reunited with his wife and children. It is likely that other Fenians imagined new opportunities for themselves in this new land. (John Boyle O'Reilly, however, saw Australia as a place from which he might try anew to escape prison — as he had repeatedly in England.) In addition, the accounts of the evening sessions, the descriptions of the food, the obvious camaraderie among the Fenians, and the production of *The Wild Goose* are evidence that it was not an abused, dispirited, or vengeful group that arrived in Australia in January of 1868.

Convict in *Australia*

It is a matter of record, though, that some in Fremantle were very much against having the Fenians sent there. This attitude was probably promoted by 'a powerful minority of influential Protestant loyalists [who] played a key role in shaping public and official consternation about a perceived Fenian threat' (Amos 99). As there seems, in fact, to have been a much more organised outcry against the Fenians than against the rather more hardened criminals who were on the boat with them, it is probable that the Protestant loyalists feared the Fenians as anti-British political activists much more than they feared the more 'common' criminals whom they knew to be guilty of theft, rape, and murder.

The civilian Fenians arrived in Australia as probationary convicts. The probationary stage was the second stage in the process of rehabilitation: the first stage — solitary confinement for six months — had already been served by most of the Fenians, including Cashman, before they boarded the *Hougoumont*. Roughly half of a convict's sentence would be spent on probationary status, with time added or subtracted for bad or good behaviour. At the end of his sentence, the convict would be issued a 'ticket of leave' so that he might seek employment, marry, and settle down; however, he was required to carry that ticket with him at all times, observe the curfew, not change employment or move without permission, and report twice yearly to the local magistrate. As last steps, the convict received a conditional pardon and then a certificate of freedom. This final certificate brought with it a remission of sentence and restoration of civilian rights (Amos 123).

Upon arrival in Australia, most of the Fenians were assigned to work gangs on various projects in and around Fremantle, and the military Fenians, except for O'Reilly, were immediately dispersed among various road crews. In an early letter to his wife, Cashman reported that the Fenians were set to hard labour: 'breaking stones and clearing bush to make way for roads.' During one two-day period, he said, 'we killed several large reptiles' (qtd. in George Ryan np). Later, however, Cashman and some others were assigned jobs of more responsibility:

> John Flood was appointed clerk in the superintendent's office; Denis Cashman, assistant clerk to the clerk of the works; Patrick Reardon, Patrick Doran and David Joyce were assigned to the prison store; and John O'Reilly became orderly and librarian to the Roman Catholic chaplain, Reverend Thomas Lynch. (Amos 127)

This new assignment caused Cashman to write to Catherine: 'By Jove! Won't I know how to perform a bit of household work for you when I get out of jail. Washing, scrubbing, pumping, scouring, with 1,000 other etc.s' (qtd. in George Ryan np). Within a month, however, O'Reilly was sent to a road crew; but this eventually turned out well for him, as it facilitated his daring escape a year later, in February of 1869, aboard an American whaler, the *Gazelle*.

While there seems to have been no systematic or selective punishment of the Fenians, save for separating the military Fenians and placing them on road gangs, there were instances of particular injustices. A letter for O'Reilly informing him of his mother's death was withheld from him on the grounds that he had been a few minutes late reporting to the overseer's office. The overseer reportedly showed O'Reilly the black-bordered letter and told him he could have it in a half-year's time (Evans 117).

Other Fenians' infractions were often about correspondence. The prisoners could receive any number of letters but were only allowed to write one every two months. Also, convicts were not allowed to correspond with one another. As one might expect, the Fenians began to violate these prohibitions quite soon. 'Between April and November of 1868, ten letters written by Keane, Kenealy, Cody, Lahey, McSwiney, Noonan and Cashman were confiscated and fifteen letters addressed to Fogarty, Downey, Flood, Cashman, Kenealy, Walle, Brophy and Fitzgibbon were intercepted' (Amos 131). Later, Patrick Reardon, John Casey, Cornelius Keane, Joseph Noonan, and Denis Cashman were all brought up on charges of having written clandestine letters. Reardon and Casey were already in solitary confinement when the other three came to be sentenced.

> Keane received the standard punishment of three days bread and water, and Noonan probably the same, but Cashman unwisely attempted to argue his case, which only prompted the magistrate to double his sentence to six days bread and water and to swear an oath that 'by God ... he would give him a month's bread and water in a dark cell,' if Cashman appeared before him again. (Amos 134)

Cashman did, in fact, appear before the magistrate again a week later, for refusing to salute the superintendent when he entered Cashman's cell, but the magistrate chose to let the matter pass (Amos 134–135).

There were other conflicts between the Fenians and the prison officials, but on the whole, the prisoners comported themselves well enough that favourable reviews went back to the British government, which began to issue pardons for the civilian Fenians in early 1869.

> Cashman, Denis (ought to be discharged) 7 yrs '67
> [under] Men actively engaged in the Conspiracy
> but not proved to have taken part in any outrage.
> ('Cashman, Denis.' *Classification List of Fenian*
> *Convicts: Fenian Arrests and Discharges, 1866–*
> *1869*)

The recommendation for Cashman's 'discharge' is indicative of the government's thinking, at the time, that the civilian Fenians who had not been involved in violent acts or otherwise acted within a military structure could be pardoned.

Funds to support the newly freed Fenians came from partisans in both Australia and Ireland. Some — like John Flood, who received only a conditional pardon — were required to stay on in Australia and New Zealand ('Papers Pertaining to John Flood'). Others, as might be expected, chose to return to Ireland; John Casey was among them. Fifteen others, including Denis Cashman, chose to head for America; they boarded the *Baringa*, bound from Sydney to San Francisco, and sailed on 21 October 1869. The military Fenian prisoners remained in custody in Australia.

Free Man in the United States

In March of 1870, the *Suffolk*, carrying John Casey and nine other Fenians, reached Ireland, where the former prisoners received a hero's welcome. The *Baringa*'s passengers were also received enthusiastically in San Francisco.

> In the new year, on 27 January 1870, the
> Anglophobic *New York Tribune* gave the Fenians
> newly arrived in California the status of escapees
> — 'Fifteen political prisoners ... have escaped and

arrived in San Francisco.' As soon as the *Baringa* entered the Golden Gate, Captain Smith ... was notified of the fact and sent the accustomed group of worthies to escort the former prisoners around the city. Those who wished to go east, it was made clear, could comfortably do so on the Central Pacific Railroad. (Keneally 521)

Denis Cashman made his way to Boston, where he was reunited not only with John Boyle O'Reilly — now working for *The Pilot*, a Boston newspaper — but also with his wife, Catherine, and one of their children, Willie.[5]

O'Reilly, after his escape from Australia, had arrived in Philadelphia a famous man on 23 November 1869. He spoke to enthusiastic audiences in both Philadelphia and New York about his adventures, the situation of the Fenian prisoners, and the problems in Ireland; but he saw his fortune in neither city, and in January of 1870, as Denis Cashman was arriving in San Francisco, O'Reilly went to Boston. It is 'more than likely that he was drawn to Boston on account of its pre-eminence as a literary centre' (Evans 193). Within a month or two, he was on the staff of *The Pilot*. He would remain with that newspaper, eventually becoming its co-owner, until he died in 1890. During his time in Boston, O'Reilly became an internationally known author, speaker, and advocate of human rights; he not only continued to work for Irish independence and freedom for Irish political prisoners, but also championed the rights of Blacks and Native Americans.

Through O'Reilly, Cashman secured 'a position in the wholesale department of the book and publishing establishment connected with *The Pilot*'. In addition to working in the publishing department, Cashman wrote articles and editorials for the newspaper, 'being a facile writer as well as a vigorous speaker'.

After the Great Boston Fire of 1872, which destroyed the editorial and printing facilities of *The Pilot*, Cashman 'assisted materially in reorganizing the ... wholesale book department,' served as one of Donahoe's top salesmen, and was Business manager of *The Pilot*, by that time (under O'Reilly as editor-manager) 'the Bible of the American Irish,' a newspaper with well more than 100,000 subscribers nationwide. (George Ryan np)

It seems, according to city records, that Cashman left *The Pilot* about 1876. At that time, he became Superintendent of the Waste Water Department in City Hall. In city records for 1889, he is listed as a U.S. storekeeper, with an office in the Post Office building. He is listed in 1890 as an 'agent' with a residence at 5 Gordon Street, Allston, and an office at 123 Heath Street; in 1892 he is listed as employed by the East Boston Express Company; and finally, in 1895, he is labelled 'insurance,' with a home in the South End and then, in 1896, in Roxbury (George Ryan np).[6]

Cashman not only continued to write articles in the Boston papers, including *The Boston Herald*, and speak at various functions (George Ryan, n. 21 & 26, np); he was also involved in the Fenians' most daring and most successful plot against the British government — the *Catalpa* mission. John Devoy had come to America after his release from prison, but he still felt an obligation to the military Fenian prisoners in Australia whom he had helped recruit. As pardon was impossible for them, a rescue was the only way to set them free. Devoy presented the idea to Clan na Gael members in New York in 1874 and was authorised to form a committee and draw up plans. After a false start, Devoy went to Boston on his own to consult with O'Reilly. O'Reilly brought Cashman into the small circle, and plans were made to buy a whaling ship, outfit her for an actual whaling journey, and have her rescue the Fenian prisoners still in Australia.

The planners kept their group small, and only they and the ship's officers knew the actual mission. Agents were sent to Australia to alert the prisoners and plan for the escape. After a year of actual whaling, the *Catalpa*, under the command of Captain George Anthony, arrived in Australia and, in spite of some miscommunications, did, in fact, take aboard six of the seven Fenians still in custody. The seventh, who had offered to be an informer for the British some years before, was left behind for his treachery. A British gunboat, the *Georgette*, gave chase and confronted the *Catalpa*, but Captain Anthony maintained that he had no prisoners on board and, when threatened with gunfire, claimed the protection of the United States flag, as they were then on the high seas. The *Georgette* left without firing a shot, and although there was an official complaint by the British to the United States, nothing ever came of it. When the *Catalpa* landed in New York on 19 August 1876, John Devoy was there to greet her, and Denis B. Cashman covered the event as a reporter for *The Pilot* (Evans 205–206).

Cashman's other major contribution to the cause of Irish nationalism was his biography of Michael Davitt, published in 1881 and entitled *Life of Michael Davitt with a History of the Rise and Development of the Irish National Land League*. The Irish National Land League grew out of an awareness, especially on Davitt's part, that there was a great deal of difference between the ideals of the urban Fenians and the needs of the rural Fenians. 'A complex young man, [Davitt] spent time in his cell contemplating the debacle of Fenianism, and had returned to the principles of Young Ireland's late Fintan Lalor: land lay at the bottom of all Irish questions' (Keneally 602). The movement succeeded largely as a result of the use of the boycott against avaricious landlords; indeed, the word 'boycott' comes from the first landlord against whom this strategy was employed, Charles Cunningham Boycott, 'land agent at Lough Mask in Mayo. Local people refused to deal with him or take his crop in' (Keneally 608). As might be expected, *The Pilot* was one of the strongest American voices in support of this movement.

If Cashman left *The Pilot* in 1876, as city records seem to indicate, the reporting of the *Catalpa*'s arrival in New York would have been one of his last official tasks. The next major event at which he appeared must have been an especially sad one for him: he served as a pallbearer, with several other well-known Fenians including O'Donovan Rossa, at the funeral of John Boyle O'Reilly on 13 August 1890. Cashman's own death came seven years later.

> Mr. Denis B. Cashman, the well-known Irish nationalist died suddenly at his home on Worcester Street, Boston, on Friday evening ...
>
> Mr. Cashman was a man of large heart and generous impulses, warmly devoted to his native land, and firm in the friendships which he made during the common struggle for liberty in the old Fenian days. The affection with which he was regarded was shown by the large number of mourning friends who came from far and near to pay their last tribute of love at his grave.
>
> Mr. Cashman was buried on January 11 from the home of his son, Mr. William P. Cashman [then living at 40 Pomeroy Street], of Brighton, the funeral services being held in St. Columbkille's Church, and very largely attended. Among those present were representatives of the Irish Charitable and the Fenian societies, and a number of prominent gentlemen. ('Death of Denis B. Cashman' 5)

In an 'Obituary', *The Boston Transcript* announced that 'Mr. Dennis [*sic*] B. Cashman ... died of heart disease' and referred to him as 'one of the brilliant young men who "published" that unique paper, "The Wildgoose" [*sic*], on board the transport ship' (5). In Ireland, *The Waterford News* published an obituary of Cashman under the title 'Death of a Waterford Patriot' (5). He was survived by his wife, Catherine, his son, William P., then of the Probate Court in Boston, and his daughters Mary and Kathleen.

I like to think that Denis B. Cashman would be pleased to know that he was remembered in his native country and in his adopted country as 'warmly devoted to his native land', as a 'brilliant young man', and as 'a Waterford Patriot'.

Some Preliminary Notes Toward a Rhetorical Analysis of Cashman's *Hougoumont* Diary

Irish emigrant writing, both letters and diaries, has been the subject of some scrutiny during the last half-century, and most of that scrutiny has dealt with what those letters and diaries reveal about the emigrant experience. David Fitzpatrick's *Oceans of Consolation: Personal Accounts of Irish Migration to Australia* examines both the contexts and contents of several sequences or exchanges of letters between Ireland and Australia, and while Fitzpatrick eschews any specific analytical approach, he does suggest that, among other things, the letters functioned as 'token[s] of solidarity and instrument[s] of reassurance, confirming the durability of long-established familial groups' (20). In *Letters from Irish Australia*, on the other hand, Patrick O'Farrell argues that 'Both the letters they [the emigrants] wrote, and those they neglected to write, carried the same implied message: no longer was there any such place as home. Writing did not bridge the gap so much as testify to it' (8). Andrew Hassam's rhetorical study, *Sailing to Australia: Shipboard diaries by nineteenth-century British emigrants*, is a detailed analysis which attempts to answer the question: 'How did writing a diary help diarists to make sense of such a momentous and absolutely alien experience as emigration by sail, to a continent about which they very likely knew almost nothing?' (2)

Emigrants, however, were not the only ones sailing to Australia. From 1788 until 1868, ships delivered convicts from all over the British Isles to penal colonies, first to the eastern districts and later to the west. According to O'Farrell in *The Irish in Australia*, 'By the 1820s and 1830s such Irish convicts were arriving at an average rate of about 1000 a year. By the time transportation to Australia's eastern colonies ended in 1853, just on 40,000 convicts ... had been sent direct from Ireland' (23). After 1853, the convict ships sailed to Australia's western shore. Denis B. Cashman and the other Fenians aboard the *Hougoumont*, the last official convict ship to Australia, landed in Fremantle, near Perth, in January of 1868. Letters that these convicts wrote were highly restricted in number and content; however, they were more or less free to receive whatever was sent to them (incoming letters could be withheld, though, as punishment for various infractions). Those convict letters have been paid some critical attention — although not always as *convict* letters.[7] Convict diaries, on the other hand, have been often quoted but little studied. Fitzpatrick and O'Farrell, of course, did not look at diaries and, therefore, would not have looked at Cashman's. Hassam, however, acknowledges that a few convict diaries exist, and mentions Cashman's diary in particular; but he suggests that convict diaries 'are largely untypical of the experience of the bulk of transportees to Australia' (5).

The convict diary certainly is untypical. Compared to the emigrants, the convicts were, as Hassam suggests, few in number;[8] but more important is the obvious fact that, while there may have been severe economic pressures behind an emigrant's move to Australia, the convict had almost no choice whatsoever about his 'transportation'. Further, the Fenians may well have been untypical among the convicts transported to Australia. As the diaries of Denis B. Cashman and John Sarsfield Casey (both written on board the *Hougoumont*) illustrate, both in themselves and in what they record, many of the Fenians were educated and literate men. Further still, the Fenians were not, as were the emigrants, seeking a new start in a new land; nor were they, like the other convicts, being transported for various criminal activities ranging from theft to murder. They were being transported for political activities — 'felony treason,' as most of their court records indicated. They were thus being forced to leave the country that they had loved and for whose freedom they had fought. The political convict diaries are, indeed, a special case, and must be examined as such rather than dismissed as mere aberrations.

An examination of Cashman's diary in contrast to the diaries about which Hassam writes suggests that the convict diary does have a rhetoric of its own, a rhetoric different in significant ways from that of the emigrant diary. Both the convict diary and the emigrant diary begin from essentially the same impulse — to make a record of, and perhaps 'to make sense of', the voyage. Later in his study of emigrant diaries, Hassam invokes both Arnold van Gennep and Victor Turner to argue that the voyage to Australia put the emigrant in a liminal state, and suggests that 'the whole of the voyage out is a kind of liminal or threshold stage, a sacred zone into which the emigrant passes for a transitional period, a zone both spatially and temporally isolated from the secular world' (55). For the convict, the voyage must have been less of a liminal stage than for the emigrant. The emigrant knew where he was going and, however reluctantly, had chosen to go there, made plans, gone through the usual separation rituals, and boarded the ship; the Fenian convicts could not have known much more than that they were headed from a prison in England to a prison in Australia. Cashman, like most of the convicts, was already serving his prison sentence when it was decided that he should be sent to Australia; and so, with almost no preparation time — no time to do more than write his wife two letters, one of which he calls in his diary 'a very melancholy epistle' (15 October 1867) — he was placed on a ship bound for Australia.[9] Thus, although both the emigrant and the convict found themselves in transit to Australia, the convict was changing only his place, not his situation; in Australia, the convict would still be a prisoner of the Crown and, separated further from family and home, would perhaps be worse off — at least emotionally — than before.

Hassam asserts that the emigrants to Australia 'were not keen travelers and on the whole they would rather have a stayed at home; ... Emigrants were emigrants because they wanted a better standard of living' (2). In *Oceans of Consolation*, one of the sequences of letters David Fitzpatrick reproduces is from Isabella Wyly, who arrived in Australia as a penniless orphan in 1851. 'Isabella's letters bring to life a plucky, optimistic, and garrulous Dublin Protestant, courageously coming to terms with colonial life. In due course, she found a job at a drapery, married her employer, and spent the rest of her life praising God, her husband, and South Australia' (96). Although many of the political convicts stayed on in Australia and did well for themselves after serving their prison terms, the thought of a 'better standard of living' was far from their minds when they first embarked for Australia. Cashman's initial entry in his diary, on 15 October 1867, recounts his reactions to being told on 24 September that he was to be sent to Australia. He describes how 'wretched' he felt, and then conjures up 'the tearful eyes & sorrowful face of my dear Kate, — gazing at our dear children, who, want her to tell them "why their Pa does not come home" — whilst she picturing to herself the terrible distance which divides us, in her bitter sorrow kisses back the answer she would not (even to herself) dare to speak, fearing to look the dread reality in the face.' At this point, and explicitly in several other entries, Cashman, however much he maintains that he is trying to make the best of things, sees the voyage initially not as an opportunity but as a further separation from the people and the land that he loves.

Although some emigrants begin their diaries with a preliminary journey, such as that from home to the port of departure, or with the embarkation, 'the largest proportion of diaries begin ... with the actual sailing of the ship' and 'even where diaries were not started until some time into the voyage, the diarist still felt it necessary to open the diary with the beginning of the journey' (Hassam 47–49). Much of what is recorded in the first sections of these diaries is about the confusion of getting one's self and possessions aboard, getting used to shipboard life, dealing with seasickness, and setting up one's room for the voyage (59–73). Cashman begins writing on 15 October 1867, having been aboard ship for fifteen days, but he recounts very little of what the emigrant diaries tell. He does mention not succumbing to seasickness: 'Several of our men took fits — I escaped thank God.'[10] Cashman's initial entry, covering the time between the day he was informed of his transportation (24 September

1867) and the day he began writing (15 October 1867), focuses primarily on two things: his separation from his family, and his reunion with Fenian colleagues.

Cashman's first response to the news that he was being transported was to feel 'wretched [at] the thought of being sent 14,000 miles away from my dear wife and children, — from all that I love on earth' (30 September 1867). And throughout the entries describing the first week, he tells about writing home, trying to telegraph Kate so that she might come and see him before his departure, and waiting in vain for a last letter from her. 'I had the mortification to see the Anchor weighed, and the "Hougoumont" under full sail being towed out to Sea from Portland, when a few hours delay would have brought me the so earnestly wished for letter, and a last Adieu from my dear K[ate] — & Boys' (12 October 1867). The second topic of that first long entry is Cashman's delight at meeting and being able to associate with the other Fenians on board. He had been in solitary confinement for almost all of the time since his arrest in January of 1867. 'When we got on board the "Earnest" steam was up ... once on board the silent system to which ... I had been rigorously subject, totally exploded — by jove didn't we talk, shake hands, and enjoy the pleasure of hearing each other talk' (30 September 1867). And throughout this first entry and the diary in general, Cashman often notes conversations with this or that person.

Although such an activity as 'talk' might seem mundane (and is certainly not a point of emphasis in emigrant diaries), to Cashman it is extremely important for two reasons. The first, obviously, is that he had not had anyone to talk with for more than half a year. The second, and somewhat less obvious, reason is that he and the others had been forced to take this journey far from home and family, and so the new and renewed friendships would be a source of mutual support for all the Fenians on the ship. During the journey, Cashman would write a poem, 'Friendship', depicting the importance of the shipboard friendships. The poem concludes:

> Oh, Friendship! Thou'rt a priceless gem: —
> Aye! Dearer far than brightest gold:
> Thy rays can glad the heart of him
> Whom worldly riches ne'er consoled.

In addition, Cashman's growing friendship with John Boyle O'Reilly would help the latter. O'Reilly, who had several times attempted to escape from prison, believed that the Fenians could seize the *Hougoumont* and sail her to freedom. He was dissuaded from this plan, and as Thomas Keneally suggests, 'Cashman had moral strength and would play an almost immediate role in soothing O'Reilly's desperation.'[11]

One of the first things the emigrants did once aboard ship, and then wrote about in their diaries, was arrange their space. Whether in cabin or steerage, the emigrants arranged their belongings and often referred to their spaces as 'snug cabins' or 'floating homes' (63–68). In fact, Hassam argues that 'Two of the most important actions which permitted a sense of individual agency were the creation of accommodation space as home and the contesting of social space' (144). Although Cashman briefly mentions sleeping arrangements and mealtime routines, there is no suggestion in his diary that he thought of the *Hougoumont* as home. Regardless of the increased privileges — walking the deck, talking with friends, watching the sunset or sunrise, smoking, and the like — the ship was still a prison ship and was taking the Fenians to yet another prison. But Cashman also wrote very little about the political aspect of his current situation;

he and the others had been warned against putting anything in writing that could be seized, examined, and used as evidence against them. Surely they must have talked about those things among themselves, as they talked about seizing the ship, but there are only the vaguest hints of such topics in Cashman's diary.[12] The two important actions which did give the Fenians 'a sense of individual agency' were their evening song- and story-fests and the creation of their newspaper, *The Wild Goose*, both of which will be discussed in due course.

Having started their diaries, the emigrants then faced the problem of what to write about the voyage — or, as Hassam puts it, the problem of 'keeping the story running' (74–106). Entries for many of the days are very similar and include only details of weather, speed, and course. In Cashman's diary, too, there are many days for which the only entry is on one or more of those topics. Hassam further states that the diaries tend to be informational, almost scientific, in recording data, or experiential, describing what the narrator did in the episode being recorded (78). The informational data about the ship's course and progress or about fish, birds, porpoises, turtles, albatrosses and so on appear in Cashman's diary as they do in the emigrant diaries. The emigrants' experiential segments include descriptions of catching sharks and turtles, witnessing drownings or funerals, and participating in various social events (and scandals) that took place. Cashman, too, reports seeing dolphins, petrels and albatrosses, helping to catch a shark and seeing a turtle caught, and watching a funeral.

On a convict ship, however, there are kinds of experiences to be described that do not as often find their way into emigrant diaries. Cashman recounts several disciplinary actions he witnessed. On 1 January 1868, 'some of the Convicts broke into the ships stores ... and abstracted several articles (provinder) one of them has been sentenced to be flogged tomorrow.' The next day, 'All hands piped on Deck at 10 o.c. to be present at the punishment — I could not look at it — so John, Jack, Old Joe, and I talked & smoked till we got below again — the man received 3 doz[en lashes]' (2 January 1868). Other experiential entries in Cashman's diary describe the organisation (24 October 1868) and subsequent presentations of evenings of songs and stories, and he includes complete programmes for seven such evenings and refers to several others in passing. Another entry describes the meeting (5 November 1868) that resulted in the shipboard newspaper, *The Wild Goose*, and subsequent entries tell of its production, contents, and oral readings. Several of the poems that appeared in *The Wild Goose* are appended to the diary.

The combination of the informational and experiential entries in Cashman's diary is particularly interesting, as it reveals his changing state of mind during the voyage. Other than marking the weather and noting lands or ships sighted as they sail past them, Cashman records little navigational information through the month of October. Toward the end of October, he does make occasional references to the speed of the ship, and on 15 November 1867 he records that at '10 o.c. (4 bells) of AM we crossed the line just now'. On 25 November 1867, however, he records, for the first time, the complete details of latitude, longitude, ship's speed, and distance travelled; and he continues this record throughout the remainder of the voyage. On 22 December 1867, he reports, 'We are all wishing most anxiously for the termination of the voyage'; on Christmas Day he says that he feels 'the day is not so far distant when I shall again press them [Kate and the boys] to my bosom'; and on 7 January 1868, just before landing at Fremantle, he reports that he and his friends have been 'conjecturing as to what sort of place our new abode will be — when we are to regain our liberty — and chalking out our future modes of life, my only hope is to earn money with as much expedition as possible and have my dearest K[ate] and dear boys with me.' The increased attention to navigational data and consideration of plans for the future indicate that Cashman has come from his initial despair to a point at which he can hope Australia will provide the means of reunion with his family.

In addition to noting navigational data, the emigrants also paid close attention to their fellow passengers. Hassam observes that 'for the true genealogist the passenger lists found in the diaries are the real strata of immigration' (107), and he spends a chapter discussing what he calls 'passenger sketches'. These emigrants, however, were, for the most part, travelling with people they had never met before, and so keeping lists of the other passengers and recording anecdotes about them gave the diarists something to write about. Moreover, as these passengers might well be separating in Australia, recording who and what they were was an integral part of and particular to the diary of voyage itself. The Fenians, if they had not actually known one another before boarding the *Hougoumont*, generally knew about one another. Cashman spends very little space discussing the characteristics of his fellow prisoners. He does mention that O'Reilly was initially reluctant to participate in the evening entertainments (24 October 1867), and he also tells us that Sheehan gave excellent comic recitations (26 and 29 October, 20 November 1867); otherwise, he relates the activities in which they engaged, his own personal feelings, or, increasingly, the progress of the ship. He says almost nothing about the other convicts; they were outsiders and socially 'below' the Fenians. He also says little about the ship's crew; they were England's representatives, and — like the non-Fenian convicts, in a way — outsiders and not to be trusted. It does seem, though, that the Fenians got along well with the authorities; Cashman records very few punishments meted out to the Fenians.[13]

Within the context of experiential and informational entries, Hassam remarks that the 'emigrants think, see, and speak, they describe events, but only rarely do they initiate what they regard as significant actions — in most cases they are acted upon by the ship or the agents of emigration' (142). One might expect the convict diaries to contain even less 'significant action' than the emigrant diaries, as the convicts were there as prisoners and could be flogged or put in chains for the least infraction. To some extent this is true. But there are some significant actions that Cashman does report — and some that he does not. In the latter category are all of the political discussions in general, and the discussions of the possibility of seizing the ship in particular. Sometimes Cashman mentions talk of home and family (e.g., 10 October 1867), and sometimes he just reports that they talked (e.g., 13 October 1867). As noted above, Cashman could not record those conversations because such records could have been used against him by the authorities.

Cashman, however, does record two significant actions that the convicts took which made the journey more tolerable for them. The first was the establishment of a series of evening concerts and story-tellings. These evenings not only kept them busy with both the rehearsals and the performances themselves, but also gave them an emotional outlet. Their songs and poems and stories were about everything from loved ones left behind to the political situation in Ireland; in fact, the Fenians closed every concert with everyone singing 'Let Erin Remember'. The convicts' second significant action was to establish a shipboard newspaper with materials supplied by Father Delany.[14] *The Wild Goose* appeared seven times during the voyage and was, as well as a way of occupying the time, another outlet for personal and political emotions. Although seldom if ever overtly revolutionary, the essays and poems in *The Wild Goose* displayed a sympathy for the current state of Ireland and for political prisoners like those aboard the *Hougoumont*, and also commented on injustices perpetrated by the English government. Both the evening concerts and *The Wild Goose* were especially significant in that they allowed the convicts to express not just personal but political feelings, in a situation in which it was somewhat dangerous to do the latter. Ironically, the Christmas issue of the paper, its last number, was so popular that the captain and the officers wanted copies, and Cashman reports that he and the others were busy copying for several days (31 December 1867 through 3 January 1868).

As the emigrants' journey drew to an end, their diary entries focused on the Australian coastline. Hassam discusses the ways in which they perceived this new land, arguing that their 'descriptions' of the Australian coast are fundamentally shaped by the country from which they had sailed (161–191). Cashman, who spent a long paragraph describing the London buildings he passed as the gunboat *Earnest* took the Fenians to the *Hougoumont* (30 September 1868), says nothing about the Australian coastline. As the *Hougoumont* was sailing from west to east, directly into Fremantle from the Indian Ocean, there may not have been much coastline about which to write. In addition, Cashman was not looking toward a new home, as were the emigrants, but toward a new prison, and he might well have been less enthusiastic about arriving in Australia — speculating, perhaps, that the relative freedom he and the others had enjoyed aboard ship might be succeeded by a more restricted life ashore. In fact, Cashman ends his diary on 8 January 1868, a full day before arriving in Fremantle harbour.[15]

In the final section of his book, Hassam discusses the ways in which the emigrants end their diaries (192–200). He finds two common aspects in these diaries: on one hand, there is commentary about shipboard rituals, the activities of the crew to make the ship ready for landing; and on the other hand, there are descriptions of the activities of the diarists themselves as they prepare to disembark (195). Cashman makes a brief remark about 'Anchors are getting ready — cables coming out from lockers — and all preparations being made for Fremantle' (8 January 1868) and leaves it at that. In addition to discussing the copies of *The Wild Goose* made for the ship's officers and commenting briefly on the last concert, Cashman spends the bulk of the last two entries speculating about the future. At the end of the 7 January 1868 entry, he says, 'my only hope is to earn money with as much expedition as possible and have my dearest K[ate] and dear boys with me where-ever I may pitch my tent as quickly as I possibly can — God grant that my ardent wish be accomplished,' and at the end of the 8 January 1868 entry, he says, 'as this is all I shall write at sea — I will (to make it more impressive) finish by praying God to bless my dearest Kathleen & my little boys — Denis.'[16]

Saying that this is the last entry he will write, and ending it with his name, certainly falls within the formulae that Hassam delineates for the closings of emigrant diaries; but the focus on Kate and the boys looks back to Ireland as well as ahead to Australia in ways that an emigrant diary usually did not. In fact, although Cashman thought of Australia as a place in which he might earn his freedom and then be reunited with his family, when he received a pardon in 1869, he sailed very soon thereafter for the United States and made his way to Boston, where he was reunited with his family. Some of his fellow Fenians, John Flood among them, stayed in Australia and built successful lives, careers, and families there. Others, including John Sarsfield Casey, returned to Ireland. It is interesting to speculate that Cashman and the others who went to America could not stay in Australia precisely because it had been a prison for them and therefore represented everything they had fought against. Their reasons for not returning to Ireland are less clear. Perhaps, like Hassam's emigrants to Australia, these former convicts became emigrants to America in search of a 'better standard of living' (2). We do know that they did not desert the Fenian cause; Cashman, O'Reilly, and others continued to work for Ireland's freedom from their new home in Boston.

There is an aspect of the Cashman diary that has few parallels in Hassam's emigrant diaries and deserves mention on that account as well as for its own merit. That Cashman had a sense of humour (albeit sometimes an ironic humour) is evident from a number of entries in his diary. He mentions, for example, a letter from Kate that he received at Millbank Prison, and reports that he 'opened it (Some of the prison officers having spared me the trouble of breaking the seal)' (24 September 1867). When he and the other Fenians are being transferred from the prison to the *Hougoumont*, he reports that they 'for some time stood the scrutiny of the spectators who gathered 'round, I presume to see for themselves what Species of Animal the Fenians resembled' (30 September 1867). About a convict who was caught stealing and 'sentenced ... (as he was a slovenly fellow) to be washed & scrubbed, after being confined for 2 hours in the water closet & pumped on,' Cashman remarks, 'I believe it will have a beneficial effect' (13 November 1867). And when O'Reilly compliments Cashman on the artwork he has done for *The Wild Goose*, Cashman says in the diary, 'I believe he has good taste' (19 December 1867).

To a large extent, what Hassam says about the last phases of the emigrant diary could apply to the rhetoric of the emigrant diary as a whole. Hassam argues that when 'emigrants wrote the coastline as a narrative, they were looking to write a narrative that mirrored their own desires' and that the emigrants' perceptions of the Australian coastline were shaped by their nineteenth-century British expectations; they looked for ways in which Australia was both like and unlike the Britain they had left (182–184). 'Clearly what would suit most nineteenth-century British emigrants would be a coastline that could be read through a conflation of both narrative paradigms, with the end point a kind of British fairyland, a destination/destiny that is not only naturally beautiful but is providentially a British colony' (184). In other words, what the emigrants saw and how they judged what they saw was predicated upon the nineteenth-century Britain from which they had emigrated. To extend this argument to the diary as a whole suggests that the way in which they wrote the whole voyage is inextricably tied in with the Britain whence they had come and their notions of a 'good life' in that cultural context. Australia may have been, for them, Britain, only better — an unspoiled (British) New World.

Cashman could not have seen Australia from that viewpoint. He had not wanted to leave Ireland and, when notified in Millbank Prison that he was about to be shipped to Australia, might well have stayed in prison there had he been given the choice. Moreover, in his cultural world-view, England was an oppressor, and the land to which he was now going was another of the oppressor's prisons. Thus, the voyage to Australia, the liminal or transitional stage between Britain and the New World, was, for Cashman, quite different than for the British emigrant. His diary, as a result, focuses on what he feels is a wrenching separation from his family and on the camaraderie of the Fenian fellowship aboard the *Hougoumont*. As the voyage progresses, his increased attention to navigational data and his plans to make a life for himself and his family in Australia indicate his adjustment to his changed sentence. The purpose of writing the diary, for Cashman, was not just to make sense out of the voyage, as Hassam says about the emigrants, but to find some hope in the voyage. The emigrants were heading for a new life in a state of hope; the Fenians were heading to a new prison and had to find some cause for hope in their new situation. The rhetorical structure of Cashman's diary is, then, a direct result of his being a Fenian prisoner first and on a ship bound for Australia second.

The *Hougoumont* Poems and Others

The diaries kept aboard ship by Denis B. Cashman and John Sarsfield Casey, the 'diary' written after the voyage by Thomas McCarthy Fennell, the production of seven issues of the shipboard newspaper, *The Wild Goose*, and the journalistic careers of John Boyle O'Reilly, John Flood, and Cashman after their Australian incarceration are ample proof that this band of Fenians was a literate group. Although O'Reilly is the only one remembered as a poet, several of the others — especially Flood, Cashman, and Edward Kelly — tried their hands at poetry as well.

The twenty-five poems that were presented in *The Wild Goose* have been integrated into their appropriate places in Cashman's diary. Of those twenty-five, only O'Reilly's 'Farewell', 'The Old School Clock' and 'The Flying Dutchman' saw wide publication before or afterwards; and their official published forms are all somewhat different from the forms in which they appear here. As a group, the twenty-five *Wild Goose* poems range from the sentimental to the political and fall into several categories. It is certainly

possible to divide *The Wild Goose* poems in other ways than
I have, but in discussing them here I looked more at theme
than at topic or chronology.

Overtly political poems include O'Reilly's 'Farewell' and
'The Green', Kelly's 'Prison Thoughts' and 'Prison Thoughts
II', Flood's 'Cinderella', 'Cremona' and 'Christmas
Garland', and Cashman's 'Friendship'. All of them, except
Flood's 'Cremona', are topical or occasional poems into
which are woven pro-Irish feelings. In 'Farewell', O'Reilly
links the Irish situation with the Israelite captivity in Egypt,
and in 'The Green' he moves from praising the colour to
predicting Ireland's freedom. Kelly's 'Prison Thoughts' was
originally written in Millbank Prison and states that he
suffers 'a living death ... for the right'. However, in 'Prison
Thoughts II', written aboard the *Hougoumont*, there is a
more hopeful tone: Kelly says that 'Hope, soft whispering,
bids me not despair,' comments that sweet are 'our prospects
to converse,' and, acknowledging that strife has taken place
in Ireland, concludes:

> Soft spirit's whispers fall upon my ear
>   By orange-scented gales borne o'er the foam;
> Thy friend in glory lives, be of good cheer!
>   Thou yet should meet him in a happier home.

Cashman's 'Friendship' is a celebration of the power of
friendship in their current situation. Flood's 'Cinderella'
disguises a political poem as a love ballad; his 'A Christmas
Garland' refers to the glory of the Brigade and welcomes
Christmas in spite of the present condition; and his
'Cremona' is a narrative poem, a story of the Brigade that
glorifies Irishmen's service in continental wars and ends with
'a fervent prayer ... / To heaven for one such victory at home
oer Ireland's foes.'

Four other poems, Flood's 'Live It Down', 'Holly Leaves' and 'Welcome Merry Christmas' and O'Reilly's 'A Merry Christmas', are also political, but much less overtly so than the previous group. Flood's 'Live It Down' urges the addressee to have courage and 'live down' slanders and other abuses from foes; the poem is dedicated to O'Reilly and was meant to raise his spirits. There are no specific political comments in the poem, and it is only the dedication to O'Reilly that makes it political. Flood concludes the poem:

> Still forward — calm and self-reliant,
> Disdainful of the little mind;
> Of scoffing ignorance defiant,
> Aside not looking nor behind.
> Still persevere in right forever;
> Perseverance wins the crown.
> Right ever conquers — wrong will never;
> Courage brother! Live it down.

Flood's 'Holly Leaves' and 'Welcome Merry Christmas' are both oriented more toward the holiday than his 'Christmas Garland', mentioned above, but both contrast the present Christmas to ones past in Ireland and thereby have political connotations. O'Reilly's 'A Merry Christmas' also contrasts the present Christmas to ones in Ireland, but concludes by saying that 'Though we spend the day / Within a prison ship' they should be gay and 'ne'er forget in after years / Our Christmas on the sea.'

Quite a few of the poems, ten in all, are 'memory' poems, recalling people, events, places, and times from the past. O'Reilly's 'Mary' and Flood's 'To — ', 'Louisa Hayden' and 'Kate' all refer to specific people, and O'Reilly's 'Erring Ones' and 'A Mother's Love' may well be based on his love for his own mother but are worded to apply to mothers in

general. Two of Flood's poems, 'Hallow E'en' and
'Christmas Eve', recall holidays in Ireland, making only a
slight reference to spending those holidays in 1867 aboard
the *Hougoumont*. Two of O'Reilly's poems, 'Memory' and
'The Old School Clock', recall a specific place or time: the
former is about the poet's youth along the Boyne and about
Mary, while the latter is about the clock that stood in his
schoolroom.

There were two straight narrative poems published in *The
Wild Goose*, and both of them were written by O'Reilly.
'Christmas Night' is the story of the North Wind's journey
on Christmas night, and O'Reilly tells how the North Wind,
after looking in windows which reveal happy scenes of the
holiday, finds a prisoner in a cell and eases the prisoner's
mind with thoughts of youth, home, father, and mother until
'penitent tears gushed freely forth as he raised his soul to
God' for forgiveness. 'The Flying Dutchman' is based on the
well-known legend, and O'Reilly characterises the captain as
a blasphemer who tells the stormy ocean, 'I care not for thy
Maker's smile — I care not for His wrath.' For his
blasphemy, the captain, ship, and crew are cursed to 'sail
forever on the deep, by angry tempests hemmed!' This poem,
like 'The Old School Clock', is one of O'Reilly's best known,
but the version here differs somewhat from the version
published in his collected works.

The final *Wild Goose* poem has the twin distinctions of
being the only one which is untitled and the only one which
is humorous. One of the shortest in the collection, the
untitled poem was written by Kelly and suggests that the
classical poet would do better drinking 'what's imbibed by
the staff of the "Goose"' than the wine he is used to
drinking.

The next five poems come from Cashman's diary and
from the book of poetry that was donated to East Carolina

University as part of the Cashman papers; none of them appeared in *The Wild Goose*. The three poems from the diary include an untitled poem by Thomas McCarthy Fennell that may have been the first page of the diary. The page has been damaged over the years, but the poem is about exile, dying for Ireland, and hope for freedom. Below the poem is a dedication to Denis Cashman. The second poem is entitled 'To Denis B. Cashman, Esq.' in the hope that 'he will remember the few bright traits, and forget the many faults and foibles of his friend', and it is signed by John Boyle O'Reilly. The poem is about maintaining hope and looking 'onward and upward'. This poem is a testament to the friendship that grew between the two men during the trip. Cashman's 'Tramp! Tramp! Tramp!' is the last poem in the diary and was written in Millbank for his son, Willie, after Cashman had heard that the 'times were stirring at home'. It is a poem which extols the possibility of victory. The two poems from the poetry book which I have reproduced here are O'Reilly's ['The French Prisoners'] and ['The Dead Who Died for Ireland'], neither of which has a title in Cashman's book, but which, in later publications, have carried the bracketed titles. The former is a homage to the French prisoners who died in Dartmoor early in the century, and the occasion of the poem was the erection of a tombstone for them, an event that occurred while O'Reilly was imprisoned in Dartmoor. This poem is also interesting as O'Reilly has written 'Now, Denis, eh?' after his signature. The full meaning of this inscription probably died with Cashman and O'Reilly, but it would seem, along with 'To Denis B. Cashman, Esq.', to be additional evidence that what had begun as a rocky acquaintanceship had become a true friendship during the voyage. The latter poem, ['The Dead Who Died for Ireland'], is an exhortation to modern Irishmen not to forget or cease to strive to fulfil the purpose of those who have already died trying to gain Ireland's freedom.

The rest of the poems in Cashman's poetry book include such well-known pieces as Edgar Allen Poe's 'The Bells' and Lord Macauley's 'Horatius [at the Bridge]' and other, lesser-known poems by people who were not on the *Hougoumont* and were not writing about the Fenian cause. It is not clear why these poems were copied into the book, but it may well have been because they were favourites or because someone, presumably Cashman, wanted to make sure he knew them for a recitation. I have chosen not to reproduce them here.

The next three poems are from John Flood's notebook. The first, O'Reilly's 'To John Flood, Esq.', like O'Reilly's similar poem dedicated to Cashman, bears witness to the friendship that grew between the two aboard the *Hougoumont*. O'Reilly enjoins Flood to recall 'the many pleasant (and busy) days we spent together over our little "Wild Goose".' The poem ends, 'We'll live as brothers ever, John, / Though severed we may be.' The other two poems, 'The Wild Geese' and 'My Star', are by Flood. The former, like Flood's 'Cremona' (discussed above), names various battles in Europe and America in which the 'Wild Geese' who fled Ireland fought, and asserts in the end that the Wild Geese are returning to Ireland. The latter — perhaps written aboard the *Hougoumont*, as it mentions moonlight 'on the deck below' — tells of a star which had once inspired him and inspires him again. While not a part of the Cashman papers, the poems in the Flood notebook are obviously a part of the Fenian experience and the *Hougoumont* voyage.

The last group of poems, which I see as a legacy of the Fenian experience and the *Hougoumont* voyage, are all by Cashman and O'Reilly. Two of them, Cashman's 'Robert Emmet' and O'Reilly's 'The Patriot's Grave', were written to honour the Irish patriot and martyr, Robert Emmet (1778–1803), who led a rebellion in 1802–1803 and is remembered for his final speech, which concluded: 'Let no man write my epitaph ... [until] my country takes her place among the nations of the earth, then, and only then, let my epitaph be written' (Madden 3). The next poem, O'Reilly's 'The Bombay', was written as the *Bombay* sailed into Delaware Bay with O'Reilly aboard, delivering him to the freedom of an American life. Three Cashman poems, 'Why Fear to Die', 'Nature's Book' and 'A Vision', were published in Boston newspapers during Cashman's lifetime in Boston and reinforce the religious sentiments of the diary. The final poem, 'Tribute of a Co-Mate in Exile', was Cashman's tribute to John Boyle O'Reilly at the dedication of the O'Reilly monument in Boston. His comments about O'Reilly seem a fitting conclusion to this section of the book.

For the *Wild Goose* poems, some of the poets took on pseudonyms; thus, 'Suir' is Denis B. Cashman, 'Laoi' is Edward Kelly, and 'Binn Éider' is John Flood (I have also added the correct names in parentheses after each pseudonym).

The quality of the poems varies widely. At one extreme are the simple poems like Flood's 'Louisa Hayden', with its four-line stanzas, AAAB rhyme-scheme, and predominantly iambic meter:

> Oh, once I loved a maiden
> Darling sweet Louisa Hayden,
> And my lip was honey laden
> And as happy as a dream.

The simple structure and straightforward sentiments of Flood's poem are found in others, most notably all of the 'memory' poems and Cashman's three 'religious' poems discussed above. But the occasion of most of these poems, written aboard a prison ship headed for Australia and written by men who knew little of their fate there, makes their simplicity a poignant reaction to their current situation.

The political poems tend to be more complex in structure, poetic style, and theme; and of the political poems, O'Reilly's are perhaps the most complex. The extended metaphor in 'The Green', the long line of ['The French Prisoners'] with its caesura, and the varied structure of 'The Patriot's Grave', O'Reilly's poem for Robert Emmet, are all quite sophisticated. The first section of 'The Patriot's Grave' has three four-line stanzas, each line six metrical feet (strong beats) long, in rhymed couplets. The second section is two stanzas long; the lines are shorter, are mostly in iambic trimeter, and have an AABCCB rhyme-scheme. The third section contains nine stanzas that are mostly in iambic pentameter and have an ABAB rhyme scheme. The last section contains twelve rhymed couplets, and each line has six metrical feet.

Although O'Reilly was to win lasting fame as a poet, Cashman's political poems, especially 'Robert Emmet' and 'Tribute of a Co-Mate in Exile', are equally ambitious. Cashman calls 'Robert Emmet' a narrative ballad, but he does not stay with a strict ballad meter or rhyme: he extends the length of the stanzas and varies the rhyme-scheme from rhymed couplets (AA, BB, CC, etc.) to an interwoven pattern (for example, ABAABB in one case and AABCCCB in another). This poem is the longest in the collection. Cashman's poem for O'Reilly is much shorter and much more regular: seven stanzas are six lines long, one is eight lines long, and the concluding stanza is four lines long, and all of them are in rhymed couplets.

The theme of all of the patriotic poems — Cashman's, O'Reilly's and the rest — is Ireland's freedom and the sacrifices that have been made and are to be made by the people fighting for that freedom.

The Cashman diary gives the reader an insight into day-to-day life aboard a prison ship and into the mind and heart of the man who wrote it. The poems, on the other hand, are more of an emotional and patriotic statement from several men who felt their exile keenly for both personal and patriotic reasons. Taken together, they are a marvellous historical document and an impressive literary presentation as well.

The *Hougoumont* Diary and the *Wild Goose* Poems

Convict Ship 'Hougoumont'
At Sea (near mouth of English Channel)
15th October 1867

'The Wanderer far from those he loves, and all his heart
    holds dear,
Oft pauses as he onward roams, to check the rising tear;
When thoughts of home, and byegone days, come
    crowding o'er his brain,
How sweet the voice within that says, hope on we'll meet
    again.'

On Tuesday the 24th of September, whilst very busily
employed at the (to me) very disagreeable occupation of
picking 'coir', I heard steps approach along the corridor

and halt opposite my cell door; instantly the Iron Gate and massive wooden door of my cell were flung open, and the order 'Stand at ye gate' given. I, glad of anything that would even for a moment thwart the monotony, or break the wretched grave-like silence of the place, immediately came to 'attention' by the door, and found my visitors to be Head Warder 'Handy' and some Warders of lower grade. Then for the first time I learned, that I was to be sent to Australia. I received the news with a very bad grace, and protested in the strongest terms against being sent, — but recollecting that I had no voice in the matter, and that go I should, I strove to make the most out of it, and drown the bitter feelings which filled my breast, by fiercely working at, or rather tearing the tough coir. — I really felt wretched, — the thought of being sent 14,000 miles away from my dear wife and children, — from all that I love on earth; with the fact staring me in the face, that I should not again for years see them, caused me to feel an acute agony, that I never before felt; and plunged my whole being into the deepest melancholy. — Imagination used to conjure up before me the tearful eyes & sorrowful face of my dear Kate, — gazing at our dear children, who, want her to tell them 'why their Pa does not come home.' — whilst she picturing to herself the terrible distance which divides us, in her bitter sorrow kisses back the answer she would not (even to herself) dare to speak, fearing to look the dread reality in the face. — In this most trying hour of my life, when all other resources failed, I prostrated myself before my Maker, and in prayer, found a soothing relief; the softening influence of which calmed my thoughts, and caused me to look with altered feelings, and a more hopeful eye on the before, so much dreaded future. — On the evening of this day I was allowed to write home, and I fear if I penned my letter in accordance with the tenor of my feelings; it was a *very* melancholy epistle, and not within the style in which I should have written — however, I now forget what I said. Next morning at exercise (i.e., pumping water) I was informed that Stanley, Jack Walsh, Power & a lot of the new arrivals from D. Ward were also to be sent; this was good news, and I thought, that after all, the affair didn't look so black as at first I anticipated, especially as a few dear friends were to go, with whom I could kill the tedium of the voyage and the exile in Australia.

During the following three days my mates and I were in a fidgeting state of impatience to know who were, and were not going, whether we should receive letters, visits, [squiggle, probably an 'etc.'] — and in this state we were doomed to remain, for until the morning of our departure we could not learn who our Companions were to be. At the end of the three days — on Saturday — whilst at exercise I was handed a letter; of course I knew from whom it was, and with feelings of mingled pleasure & expectancy I opened it (Some of the prison officers having spared me the trouble of breaking the seal) and was gladdened with the news which it contained that my dear Kate & boys were all well and that she would start to see me immediately on hearing from me [squiggle for 'etc.']. — I instantly applied for permission to write again, as I was entitled to write two letters, one on account of leaving, and the other by right (six months having elapsed since I last wrote; in this I was doomed to the most bitter disappointment I had yet experienced, for on making application to the Head Warder, He informed me that it was too late to write, as it was expected that we were to be sent on board the ship on Monday. I then asked permission to telegraph that Kate might start immediately, that I might be consoled with a visit and last embrace from her whom I most loved on earth before starting on my long journey.

Next morning Stanley and I were marched together thro' the intricacy of corridors & pentagons till we arrived at the Governors Office. I was here told that even a telegram would be of no avail, that it would not reach in time, but that I might write another letter, and on retracing our steps to C. Ward Stanley told me that he wasn't going, — this was very bad news, and again plunged me into the melancholy & despondency which I at first felt, but thank God, in the remedy which I at first tried; I again found relief and consolation — After fervent prayer on that night, I felt quite reconciled. — Next day (Sunday) I again wrote home: — and was re-invested in the order of the Scapular. — I received a pair of Sclrs [probably an abbreviation for 'Scapulars'] together with a present of a Prayer Book & Rosary from Father Zenetti, this morning I was quite certain that Power & Stack, [squiggle for 'etc.'] were to be sent, they being enrolled with me. — this day during dinner hour I had to don the raiment served out for the voyage, — which I thought presaged a speedy departure.

Monday 30th Sept^r — I was roused at about 3.45 this morning and desired to dress in the new clothes, that not a moment was to be lost, — so I hurriedly got into them, & marched into the Corridor where I was joined by Jack, & Bains, we were then marched into D. Ward. — we were here joined by 21 others, and marched in single file to the reception Ward, where we had an augment of 6 more — here we were placed in a Cell — and whilst breakfast was being served I indulged in the first chat for 9 months — I now heard for the first time that my friend John F, was going which considerably cheered me — after a hurried breakfast & a hearty shake of the hand from every Gael who hove in sight, we were placed in a rank along the Ward to answer a Roll call, after which, we were chained together (ten in a gang) our lads being all separated and mixed with ordinary convicts, — I had the misfortune to be chained to a foxy animal, who growled like a bear if I changed a jot from my course to shake hands with a friend fore or aft. — We were then marched out of the Prison, across the quay, and on board the gun boat 'Earnest' on route for the 'Hougoumont' lying at Shearness, which Ship was to convey us on our long journey, away from our dear friends and Country, to our Exile in Western Australia, — Crossing the Quay before embarkation, I cast a look behind, and even almost now feel the pleasurable sensation which filled me, when I found myself on the outside of this gloomy, & grim looking pile, with its Towers, Iron Windows & cold, frowning aspect, where I had spent the most miserable seven months of my life, — When we got on board the 'Earnest' steam was up, and after a few moments she got under weigh, — once on board the silent system to which, since my arrest on the 11th January I had been so rigorously subject, totally exploded — by jove didn't we talk, shake hands, and enjoy the pleasure of hearing each other talk — the thing was new to a lot of us, and we enjoyed ourselves to the best of our inclinations.

Passing down the 'Thames' I caught a glimpse of several of the principal buildings in that Quarter of the City, I certainly had a splendid view thro' the small circular window of the cabin in which we were stowed of the 'House of Commons' & 'Lords' — I thought the Parliament House the most beautiful & splendid piece of

Architecture I had ever beheld, it is a chef d'oeuvre of the most florid Gothic style & embellished from its base to the summit of its lofty towers with one mass of ornament, foliage, and — beauty. The portion of Westminster bridge which I saw was also very beautiful, in fact in keeping with the style of the exquisite pyle from opposite which it crosses the 'Thames' — a little further on I saw 'Somerset House' now used for Public Offices, it is a splendid Edifice, but from the restlessness of the Animal to whom I was chained, and indeed the general rush of my friends to the small window, I was unable to see sufficient of it to impress my mind with its style. — I saw several other pretty buildings, the names of which I cannot remember.

As creature comforts are not to be despised (even by Convicts) at about 12.30 o.c. we applied to our Haversacks with which we were furnished and dined off a lump of cold meat and bread to allay the cravings of the inner man, — about 3 o.clock PM, we arrived at Shearness, and were immediately taken on board the 'Hougoumont' where we for some time stood the scrutiny of the spectators who gathered 'round, I presume to see for themselves what Species of Animal the Fenians resembled, — when arrangements had been made, and after again answering to our names, we were ordered below, where we were assigned bunks, and our locations, and formed into messes of eight men each, — All my messmates with the exception of Kelly were strangers to me, nevertheless we very shortly fraternized and became good friends. — One man from each mess was appointed Mess Captain, whose duty it was to draw provisions. There were now 36 political prisoners on board — but we expect to take on more at Portland prison to which we were bound. — A few hours after we came on board a Tug Steamer brought us more prisoners, amongst whom I recognized 7 or 8 political prisoners (Military) with whom I was in D. Ward in Millbank, they left Millbank for the public works about 3 months previously, — the poor fellows looked much altered and worn out since I last saw them, — this (30th Sept[r]) was to me an eventful day, after long months of monotony and ennui which I had at Millbank, and I was heartily glad for a change of any sort, — Out of the lot I recognized a few friends — And I doubt if we slept much this our first night at Sea. Several of our men took fits — I escaped thank God.

1st Oct[r] — ['This morning' crossed out] we were on deck at 6 AM; the morning was beautiful, — the ship sailing under full canvas, — I enjoyed the morning very much, one day having so much changed (for the better) my position, and I heartily returned the numerous greetings of my friends, The day passed off well — I had a long chat about home & friends with John Flood, and again old memories and scenes were revived; thus agreeably passed the first day. We occasionally had a fine view of Coast Scenery passing down the channel for the next few days.

2nd Oct[r] — We put into Portsmouth to get a new spar to replace one which was broken on the night, — We weighed anchor same day, and arrived at Spithead on

6th October — Dropped anchor in Portland Roads, Next day we took a good many prisoners on board, among

whom came Con Mahony, Brophy, Jack O'Reilly, & a lot more. — A Clergyman the Revd M. Delany came on board — I was glad to hear that he was going to accompany us on our voyage.

7th On this day I wrote my dear K — I trust in a more cheerful tone that I had done in my last letter, Letters were served out to several — I anxiously expected one but none came — I patiently waited for the next five days, for an answer to mine of the 7th — but in this I was also disappointed, and on the

12th Oct^r — I had the mortification to see the Anchor weighed, and the 'Hougoumont' under full sail being towed out to Sea from Portland, when a few hours additional delay would have brought me the so earnestly wished for letter, and a last Adieu from my dear K — & Boys — The 'Earnest' left us, and under a favorable breeze — we proceeded on our journey.

13th Sunday, I was on deck at 6 o.c. AM, a very fine morning, — this in reality was our first day to sea, — We had Mass on board this morning it was served by J. Casey (the Galtee Boy) we all made ourselves quite comfortable below and talked 'till morning —

14th, up at 6, went on deck immediately to enjoy the fresh sea breeze — During the 15, 16th we had some rough weather, but no accident

18th Octr We got into the Bay of Biscay today — very rough weather, ship going about 11 or 12 knots, nothing of importance occurred, except being struck by a squall & nearly upset — shipped heavy sea & had canvas torn to shreds

19th Octr We sighted a Stranger today, her bulworks crowded with Emigrants, she showed French colors, — weather still wild, ship pitching most disagreeably

20th, Another ship in sight today, — a whale seen, I wasn't on deck at the time, cleared the Bay

21st We sighted the Spanish Coast, — ship with a fair wind running about 11 knots

23rd — A Squall passed us today, no injury resulted, — great numbers of porpoises playing around the ship

24th — An escquisite Sunrise this morning, — We had a debate to-day as to the best means of killing time and amusing ourselves during the voyage — I proposed theatricals, it was agreed to but in consequence of not having sufficient room for a Stage, we abandoned the project, to substitute which I drew up a programme for a concert, which I expect will come off with eclat at 6 o.c. this evg — Jack O'Reilly and I preparing to recite 'Brutus & Cassius' but I believe the beggar doesn't take much interest in it, The weather getting extremely warm, — preserved potatoes given us to-day for the first time — we rather like them.

25th On deck early — a very early cloudy morning, slight rain, — a beautiful day — yard is square — a ship we sighted yesterday still in sight — last night's Concert a decided success. We appointed a Chairman and Vice to preserve order & arrange the proceedings

Programme

1st part

Duet	'The Last Rose of Summer'	Noonan & Cashman
Song	'Paddies Evermore'	M. Moore
Recitation	'The Spanish Champion'	M. Duggan
Comic Song	'Doolan's Ass'	Coady
Song	'The Wished for blow'	T. Fennell
do	'Freedom's War'	Keane
Recitation	'Death of Lord Edwd'	Coady

Song	'She is far from the land'	Ja^s Flood
Comic Song	'Bob Ridley'	Daly

2nd part

Song	'Lamh Dearg Aboo'	Duran
Recitation	'Gertrude of Wyoming'	Kelly
Song	'The old Willow Brook'	Brophy
do	'Far away o'er the foam'	Cashman
do	'Tell me Mary'	Noonan
do	'Castle Dalton'	Downey
do	'Beautiful Erin'	Bradley, Noon & self
Chorus	'Let Erin Remember'	

26th Oct^r — A calm morning, but Squalls expected — read over Kates letters to-day — K^d the enclosures a 100 times — our second Concert took place last evg — one of the Convicts received 48 lashes administered by Boatswain for some <u>serious</u> offence — showed no mark of suffering — prisoners cheered him at the last strike (prisoners in irons for the first time)

1st Part

Song	'Burial of McManus'	Coady
Duet	'I've wandered in my dreams'	Cashman & Noonan
Song	'Love and Duty'	Moore
Recitation	'Gertrude of Wyoming'	Kelly
Song	'Shaun o'Farrell'	John Flood

do	'Erin Machree'	Kearney
do	'Yankee Doodle'	Jack Walsh
do	'Clares Dragoons'	Bains

2nd Part

Song	[no title here]	Coady
do	'The Harp'	Geary
do	'The Old Water Mill'	Hogan
do	'General Munroe' (a card)	Sheehan
Recitation	'The fate of McGregor'	Cashman
Song	'The Bards Legacy'	Noonan
Recitation	'To be, or not to be'	Kinneally
Song	'Dolly Dunne'	Coady
do	'Ned of the Hills'	Bradley
do	'A rally for Ireland'	Lambard
Chorus	'Let Erin remember'	all

'I've wandered in dreams' greatly appreciated, Old Joe sang beautifully, — this air recalls scenes and happy memories, never to be forgotten. J. Flood sang 'Shaun O'F' in splendid style — but by jove Sheehan <u>excels</u>, he's a card, 'In came his sister' etc

27th Oct^r — Last night was terribly squally — we were struck about midnight by a squall, and roused from sleep — the 'Jib' burst in pieces — at 8 Bells (midnight) we were roused with the cry of 'Breakers ahead,' — the crew refused to go aloft — the foreyard got entangled with the shroud — great excitement on board

The island of Maderia (Portugese) in sight this morning — about 30 miles distant, — this accounts for the cry of 'breakers ahead' last night. I believe (and indeed so do all hands) that we had a narrow escape. Our concert last night as usual, some good songs sung.

28th A beautiful morning — I was on deck early. Ship running about 8 knots under square spars, — A sail in sight — twas said this was our 'Convoy,' we believe not, A whale was seen to-day, spouting water about 60 feet high. A most escquisite Sunset this evening. I watched him for about an hour sinking into the Sea, and have never before beheld anything so beautiful, the light clouds 'round the Western horizon were burnished with the most varied and beautiful tints, parts appearing like lakes of burnished gold, fringed with a luminous Silver border in parts where he peeped thro' crevices of thick cloud it looked like so many furnaces or campfires in the distance, — just as he was ['sinking' is crossed out] half emerged in the water — a ship ['appeared' crossed out] no larger than a bird appeared, glided up atop its disc — after it had disappeared — the clouds assumed their most grotesque & fanciful appearance — Some looked like kangaroos smoking short pipes — others like huge bears sitting on their haunches, & in fact the most curious animals imaginable — when the gray twilight appeared — we were piped below and are about to open our Concert for the 28 (today) as I am to appear — I had better have a rehersal

29 Octr A beautiful calm day — we are nearing the tropics — weather getting very warm — Ship doing about 5 Knots — I have to go below to <u>school</u> for two hours, being

an odd number, i.e., sleeping in top bunk (between Kelly & Bains) even numbers are to be down tomorro' — the Concert of last night was very good

Programme

1st part

Song	'The anchor's weighed'	Coady
Recitation	'The Skylark'	Duggan
Song	'King O'Toole & St. Kevin'	Moore
do	'We are all coming Sister Mary'	Dunne
do	'Erin Mavournan'	Noonan
Recitation	'The Old School Clock'	O'Reilly

This was written by himself — Thackrey
inserted it in the 'Cornhill Magazine'

Duet	'I'll Mourn the Hopes'	Self & Noonan
Song	'Remember the Glories'	Cummins
do	'The P^c he leads a happy life'	Bradley
do	'The dear little Shamrock'	Doran

2nd part

Song	'Our Irish flag'	Coady
do	'How did they pass the Union'	Kelly
Recitation	'The Geraldines'	Lombard
Song	'We meet again'	self
do	'Native Music'	Moore
Comic do	'Doolan's Ass'	Cranston
Recitation	'Fontannoy'	Kinneally
Song	'The Penal Days'	Kearney
Story	'The Stolen Pig'	Sheehan
Chorus	'Let Erin remember'	

Sheehan had us all roaring with his story, — he has a <u>refined brogue</u> — & <u>splendid delivery</u>

30th Oct^r — On Deck & washed a 6 AM — not a puff of wind, nor a ripple on the sea — ship going scarcely a knot, a great heat, about 70 degrees between decks — a sail in sight — shoals of porpoises 'round the ship — almost becalmed — a beautiful sunset — I enjoyed the first cigar today in 12 months — I occasionally get some tobacco — it's a luxury here — sternsails up last night

31st — Last night's concert came off well I have just finished one for tonight here it is

Programme

1st part

Song	'The maid of Castile'	Noonan
Rec	'Shawn O'Neill'	Kelly
Song	'Steer my Bark'	M'Sweeny
do	'Kitty O'Shaughnesy'	Doran
do	'Rich and rare'	Bradley
Rec	'The Green' (by himself)	O'Reilly
Song	'O'Donnell aboo'	Barnes
do	'Farewell to Ireland'	Riordan
Song	'The Prisoner's Hope' (by myself)	Self

2nd part

Song	'When other [Lips?]'	Doran
Rec	'The Uncle, a Mystery'	Self
Song	'The Galley Slave'	Hogan
do	'Our Irish Canon'	Kearney
do	'Jones Grave'	Lombard
Story	'The Elopement of Jack & Molly'	Sheehan
Chorus	'Let Erin Remember'	

A calm day — slight breeze. We are going to make a snap — We've preserved our wine for two days

1st Novr Last night's programme to be performed tonight. All Saints Day (we had Mass to-day) I received Communion 2nd time — Passed the Tropic of Cancer to-day — awful warm day — A meeting to-day re-newspaper — adjourned

2nd We are nearly becalmed to-day — very warm — 13 sail in sight — a beautiful day. A large shoal of Dolphins playing 'round the ship — & chasing each other through the water — 1. o.c. PM a large Shark crossed out bows, about 17 feet long — great numbers of birds flying about (I think a species of swallow [)] — 2.30 A boat put off from ship armed with a harpoon — & captured a very large turtle which was floating thro the sea — they had great difficulty in lifting him in — a beautiful evg.

3rd (Sunday) Dark morning — Running about 5 Knots, — A Stranger quite close looks like an American — heat amidships about 80° — very warm — square yards

4th A flying fish leaped on board this morning — it is almost as large as a herring with fins which stretch along its sides & open, like wings — 12 o.c. noon Shoals of flying fish darting thro' the water, like birds skiming along its surface — We chucked our chocolate overboard it was abominable — got tea instead — We got an increase of six pints of water (much needed) each mess we now have 14 per Diem — running about 10 Knots

Programme as usual this evening

5th We held a meeting to see if we could start a newspaper — the meeting was composed of Con Mahony, J. Flood, Duggan, O'Reilly, Coady, Casey, Noonan & self — we passed resolutions, appointed a Chairman & finally settled to start if we get paper. JF appointed Editor & O'R — 'sub Kelly manager — B — pD — meeting adjourned

Running about 8 Knots — wind — sails left down to bring fresh air between decks (I received Communion this morning) — No Mass — we passed a Brazilian Mail Steamer this leg homeward bound — a huge bird called a cormorant seen

6th On deck early, — land ahead — the Island of St. Antonio. One of the Cape de Verde Islands — about 30

miles off — it belongs to Portugal — shoals of porpoises around the Ship — 12 o.c. noon — we have just passed St. Antonio — about 3 miles off — waterfalls down its sides — it looks mountainous — & volcanic — 2 high cones — probably craters — a curious rock shaped like a Castle — Con K caught a large fish about 6 lbs weight — shoals of flying fish darting about — Another island to the west — 4 o.c. (8 Bells) we are now passing C[ape of] St. Vincent — between both islands — its summit is about [scratched out] feet high — I have just had a splendid view of St. Fogo or (Bravo) we are about two miles off it, it has two immense Craters one about 8000 feet high, its summit is appearing over a thick white cloud which hides a great part of it the island presents a curious appearance — covered over with hillocks, & its sides covered with lava & crusted, we passed it just now at 5 o.c. Another island appears — but we are far off it. 6.10. PM, a beautiful sunset. Fogo disappearing in the Distance — We have passed the Cape de Verde islands. 7 o.c. McG plays 'Garryowen' on Coronet — very warm between decks — our Concert about to begin

7th We had a meeting & debate as to what our paper should be called when finally we resolved to call it 'The Wild Goose' (Kelly's suggestions[)], several beautiful names were suggested, the first number is to appear on Sat[y] the 9th so I must go at the heading (a wreath of shamrocks with the name peeping thro' it) I expect to be rather busy for the voyage at it.

8th We had a tropical shower this morning very large drops — ship doing 10 Knots — preparing for a squall — the staff of the 'Goose' are hard at work all day — I have scarcely a moment to spare — printing all day, No. 6 Mess is turned into a publishing office — Last night's Concert was very good — good singing

Programme

1st Part

Comic Song	'Doolan's Ass'	Coady
Song	'The Mess Tent'	Baines
Rec	'The Vale of Cevadonga'	Self
Song	'The Black flag'	Connolly
Song	'Kentucky Home'	Hogan
Duet	'I've wandered in Dreams'	Self & Noonan
Song	'Jolly Soldiers'	Kelly
do	'Let me like a Soldier fall'	Bradley

2nd part

Song	'Gilla Machree'	Cummins
Rec	'Uncle Ned's Story' (by himself)	O'Reilly
Song	'The Young May Moon'	J. Flood
do	'Fatherland'	Downey
do	'Norah McShea'	Hogan
do (comic)	'B. Barlow'	Cranston
Chorus	'Let Erin Remember'	

very hot today — about <u>80</u> degrees — awful between decks

9th On deck at 6 Witnessed a very beautiful sunrise — ship going about 4 Knots, Stern sails going up — very warm — no more school till we get into a cooler ['latitude' crossed out] — nearing the equeator — Convicts dancing on the deck to Guitar music — rather amusing — 'The Wild Goose' made its appearance this Evening address to Readers (by J.F.) the Editor beautifully done, 'Farewell' by Jack OR — (a poem) 'Prison Thoughts' a poem by E.K. — the leader 'Home Thoughts' well written, we intend having it read for our lads at 6 o.c. — Concert postponed in consequence — I believe it to be a success

Farewell

Farewell! Oh, how hard and sad 'tis to speak
That last word at parting — for ever to break
The fond ties and affection that cling round the heart
From home, and from friends, and from country to part
But 'tis harder, when parted, to try to forget,
Though it grieves to remember, 'tis vain to regret
The sad word must be spoken, and Memory's spell
Now steals o'er me sadly. Farewell! Oh, Farewell!

Farewell to thy green hills, thy valleys, and plains,
My poor blighted country! In exile and chains,
Are thy Sons doomed to linger. Oh God! who didst bring
Thy children to Zion from Egypt's proud King,
We implore Thy great mercy! Oh, stretch forth Thy hand
And guide back her Sons to this poor blighted land.

Never more thy fair face am I destined to see;
E'en the savage loves home, but 'tis crime to love thee.
God bless thee, dear Erin, my loved one — my own!
Oh! how hard 'tis those tendrils to break that have grown
Round my heart. — but 'tis over, and Memory's spell
Now steals o'er me sadly. Farewell! Oh, Farewell!

Hougoumont, Oct 12ᵗʰ 1867　　　*JBOReilly*
　　　　　　　　　　　　　　　　　　[signature]

Prison Thoughts

Whilst to and fro my prison cell I trace
　　　The drear elliptic course with constant feet,
Thought spurns restraint, and, eager to embrace
　　　Loved friends and scenes, speeds far on pinions fleet.

Between the bars the golden sunbeams stray,
　　　And whisper stories of the world outside;
And joyous sparrows twitter all the day,
　　　As if my prison sorrows to deride.

Back in the past! I am again a child,
　　　Kneeling at mother's side in reverent prayer
Before God's awful throne. In accents mild
　　　She prays the Lord to make her boy His care.

To guide his steps, from sin to keep him free,
　　　Then teaches me the sacred page to read,
That I must bow to his all-wise decree,
　　　And always praise, and pray in hour of need.

In childhood's cloudy hour, who soothed my woe
 And kissed from off my cheek each falling tear,
And lulled me to her breast in sweet repose,
 Best friend of earthly mould, — my mother dear.

In far Acadia lies her sacred dust;
 Her sainted spirit dwells in realms of light,
Whilst I — my only hope that God is just —
 A living death must suffer for the right.
Me thinks I breathe the hallowed atmosphere
 Around that grave, and gain new strength therefrom:
My heart her cenotaph contains — writ there
 'Thy will, O God! be done, Thy kingdom come!'

       Laoi [Edward Kelly]
       Millbank, July, 1867

10th — (Sunday) Mass celebrated to-day — I organised a quire — we sang — the Congregation praised the performance — we sang some beautiful pieces — The 'Goose' greatly liked last night — it was read by O'Reilly — <u>Wine business</u> curious, a Squall passed us by this Evg — we weren't struck.

11th On Deck early at 5 AM — I had a salt water bath for the first time this morning — I relished it very much — we were allowed up by ourselves — the Grand Constellation of the Southern Cross is now visible — I haven't had the pleasure of seeing it — two sail in sight

12th — It blew hard last night — ship sailing under reefed top-sails — intense heat to-day — fully 90 degrees — we had a Concert last night as usual — I sang 'Love not' and gave a reading from 'Nicholas Nicholby' 'Do the boyshall' it was greatly liked — We got into the trade winds this Evg — excessive heat, a shoal of flying fish just passed & flocks of Petrols (Mother Curys Chickens) darting before us — Coronet playing on deck by McG — very near the line this Evg.

13th — fine morning — cooler day than yesterday — an amusing scene occurred to-day — a convict was detected stealing provender from his mess & brought before the Surgeon Superintendent, who ordered him to be tried by a Court martial of Convicts — the trial was most amusing — they sentenced him (as he was a slovenly fellow) to be washed & scrubbed, after being confined for 2 hours in the water closet & pumped on — I believe it will have a beneficial effect

14th — On Deck early to wash our clothes — A ship homeward bound passed us at 2 o.c. — Another sail in sight — Concert tonight as usual

Programme

1st Part

Song	'Erin my Country'	Downey
do	'Johnny Sands'	Moore
Rec	'Lochiels Warning'	Duggan
Song	'Fenigan Taylor'	Sheehan
do	'Young Recruit'	Bradley
do	'After the Battle'	Fennell
do	'English and Irish'	Fennell
Rec	'The Pioneer'	Self

2nd Part

Song	'They call us aliens' (by O'Reilly)	J. Flood
do	'Norah the Pride of Kildare'	Self
do	'Gra Gal Machree'	Cummins
Recitation	'French Prisoners' (by himself)	O'Reilly
Song	'The heart bowed down'	Noonan
do	'Gentle Annie'	Harrington
Comic do	'Anne O'Neill'	Cranston
Chorus	'Let Erin Remember'	

Hard at work to-day for the 'Goose' Shamrock wreath heading.

15th A beautiful morning — 10 o.c. (4 bells) of AM we crossed the line just now, blowing pretty hard — Gib sheet burst, a very large bird, supposed to be an 'Albatross' flying about ship — 5 o.c. PM wind getting down.

16th I was on deck at 4.30 AM and enjoyed a bath — very
fine morning — but very warm — the second number of
'the Goose' appeared to-day — it contained an amusing
report (by Jack) of the Cato Court-martial — a fine leader
on self-reliance (by J.F.) and a poem (The Green) by Jack
— & 'Hallow E'en' by John [Flood], — A large paddle
steamer, with double funnels, seemingly English passed us
this Evg — ship 140 miles South of the Equator this Evg.

The Green

Go seek ye the fairest tint on earth
From Nature's beauteous train;
In the gorgeous east or the snow-clad north,
Or away o'er the southern main;
'Mid the isles that vie with the land of the blest
'Neath their cloudless skies of blue;
Or search ye the pride and wealth of the west
For the fairest and loveliest hue.
Some boast of red with its glaring flaunt
And its deep ensanguined dye;
And some of the Kingly purple vaunt,
Or the blue of a Grecian sky.
But a tint there is that far above
The purple or ruby's sheen, —
Of earth are they — but almighty love
Is clothed in the beautiful green.
At Nature's birth, when her colors arose,
And her beauties were all arrayed

The bright warm green was the tint she chose,
And of green was her mantle made.
When she comes with the spring to adorn our globe
The bountiful Goddess is vain
Of the varying hues of her beauteous robe
As a maid of her silken train.
In summer, with flow'rets bright + wild
She decks out her mantle fair,
With playful grace, as a laughing child
Twines rosebuds through her hair.
In autumn she rules with her brightest glow,
When the rich, ripe fruits are seen
Where fairest their tempting beauties show —
Mid their deep dark leaves of green.
But Oh! in the winter she loves it most
When her bright gay hues are flown;
When the pride and the beauty of summer are lost
And the fruits of autumn are gone;
All fled are the joyous smiles of Spring,
Not a wild-flower even is seen;
But still round the goddess for ever doth cling
Her emerald robe of green.
Oh! fairest and best of colors of earth,
How I love the genial smile!
Thy bright warm hue in my heart gives birth
To dreams of my own Green Isle.
To my childhood's home Swift Memory runs,
O'er every well-Known scene;
Oh! deep in the hearts of her exiled Sons
Is the love of their beautiful green.
'Tis never extinguished — it never decays —
It came with their earliest breath;
'Tis a light that is holy and pure, whose rays
Are vanquished alone by death.

God grant that the dawn of the morning is nigh
When o'er liberty's ranks will be seen
Their heart-cherished Sunburst rise gleaming on high
From its glorious field of green.

JBO'Reilly [signature]

Hallow E'en

To night, my friends, with hollow mirth
We sing away our cares;
But ah! there is a woeful dearth
Of music in the airs
A smile, tis true, is on each lip,
    A light is in each eye,
As onward speeds our crowded ship,
    Beneath a brilliant sky;
A silvery ripple in her wake,
    A soft breeze in her sail,
As southward still our course we take
    From thee, loved Innisfail.
But in each voice there is a thrill. —
    A soft, sad thrill of pain,
That tells of memories, that fill
    The heart, as back again
On fancies wing, across the foam,
    We fly to those who weep,
Breathing angel prayers at home,
    For lov'd ones on the deep.

To loving wife, and lisping child —
  To maiden idolized —
To mother dear — to sister mild —
  To all belov'd and prized; —
And to our hearts, in mute despair,
  Each best lov'd one is pressed,
And lips, and eyes, and brow, and hair,
  Are kisséd and caressed.
Tis Hallow E'en; a year ago,
  Our lov'd ones softly smiled
Upon us, and with hearts aglow,
  Enraptured, and beguiled,
We listened to their voices sweet,
  And laughed, nor thought of care,
Tonight, dear friends, like seabird fleet,
  With white sails thro' the air,
Our vessel bears us far away,
  And thro' her masts the wind,
Like murmurings of those who pray,
  Breathes love from friends behind —
But still, my friends, we'll bravely sing,
  With hearts that never quail,
As onward bounds our convict ship,
  From thee, lov'd Innisfail.

Binn Éider (John Flood [signature])

[NB: Line 2 was not indented in the original.]

17th (Sunday) Mass Celebrated Quire performed 1.30, a tropical shower — very large drops — 351 miles south of the line — very warm day — Jack & I had a long chat — 'Goose' read last night greatly applauded — I'm getting up tonight's program.

18th Ship running 10 Knots — a sail in sight — I saw a Portugese 'Frigate' to-day quite close to the ship — it is a sort of shell fish of a beautifully varigated color — two sails or wings projecting high from its back gives it a pretty appearance — they are value for about £1 Stg in England — A sail in sight — 531 miles South — (South Atlantic) — Dancing on Deck — 'Patricks Day' performed on Guitar —

19th Rather rough & blustry last night. — Fore-royal top sheet carried away by a squall (at night) — ship running about 10 Knots — another court martial on the forecastle-deck to-day — the prison was charged with 1½ sticks of tobacco — the trial was conducted in admirable style — but the prisoner was acquitted — the proof not being sufficient. the Military Guard were armed with broom-sticks & staves & enforced order vict armis — the thing was very amusing — Serg & Softack & Crp[l] Pompey in command — one of our men reported for having in his possession an awl which he refused to give up — his wine stoped for 7 days — A sail passed our lee-bow — a clear sunset — All hands piped below

20th Nov^r — Ship running about 6 Knots under full canvas, square yards — heat about <u>85 degrees</u> — <u>vertical sun</u> I have thrown off my clothes to avoid being smothered — last nights programme rather good here it is

Programme

1st Part

Song	'Paddies evermore'	Moore
Song	'Lamh Dearg aboo'	Doran
Song	'Ned of the Hill'	Bradley
Rec	'Downfall of Poland'	Self
Song	'The Rising of the Moon'	J. Flood
Song	'Rally for Ireland'	Lombard
Song	'Marseilles Hymn'	Moore

2nd Part

Song	'Tell Me Mary'	Noonan
Duet	'Good Bye Sweatheart'	Self & Joe
Song	'Macreeveen Eveen'	Kearney
Rec	'Uncle Ned's Tale' 2nd p^t	O'Reilly
Song	'Fontennoy'	Brophy
Song	'Convict Ship'	Fennell
Story	'Elopement of Shaun McCarthy'	Sheehan
Chorus	'Let Erin Remember'	

The songs were sung in admirable style, but Sheehan's story licked creation.

21st — Almost Becalmed going scarcely a Knot — Calms
are very prevalent about the tropics — so we expect slow
going here — a beautiful evening — slight breeze — a sail
in sight — I felt rather in the blues to-day — thinking of
the Dear Ones at home — and have again & again read
over my dear K^s letters — went to my bunk early

22nd I went on deck early & enjoyed a bath in our large
Reservoir — weather warm — South American coast is
nearest land — it is about 250 miles distant — Cape St.
Rogue is the nearest point of it — a large school of
porpoises around the Ship — and numbers of Petrols
(chickens) about — a huge bird called a 'boobie' alighted
in the rigging — 11.30 AM land ahead (Trinadade Island)
about 10 miles off (South Atlantic) towards Evg. we came
quite close to Trinadade — its appearance was that of a
huge Mass of Rock — the day was too hazy to get a
proper view of it — I have been hard at work all day
preparing 'The Goose' for tomoro' it promises to be a
good number — this occupation pleases me very much —
it passes the time — & it takes me from my thoughts
which at times are rather gloomy, — this has been a
terrible stormy day. we got knocked about like old boots,
wind & rain against us all day — so I think the best thing I
can do is to turn in and dream of my dear K, Willy,
Arthur, and my little namesake — our sails have just been
torn to shreds — rather pleasant

23rd On Deck early — Morning gloomy — We sailed under reefed top-sails last night — Our 3rd Number of the 'Wild Goose' out this day — the leader on 'Forethought' and 'What are the wild waves saying' splendid, 'Two Days at Killarney' by Old Joe — some good poetry, I feel in good spirits to-day

Mary

I see thee, Mary, now before me
As I saw thee long ago;
Dreams of youth are rushing o'er me
With resistless rapid flow.
Time and worldly cares have found me;
Each has left its mark behind.
Still those day dreams hover around me,
Saddening treasures of the mind.

Far from childhood's house I wander,
Sorrows come and disappear,
Still when on the past I ponder
Thou art present, Mary, dear.

Scenes of boyhood — scenes of gladness —
Parents' love and friendship's ties,
Bearing mingled joy and sadness,
Now 'neath Memory's wand arise.

Crush them not, their spells will render
Truer, kinder, every heart;
Crush not feelings pure and tender,
Scenes of youth, Oh! ne'er depart.

E'en though sad, yet still I cherish
All those dreams as time flies on;
Base 'twould be to let them perish
Now that all their joys are gone.

May they still my memory fetter,
Still their spells around me cast,
Teach me to grow wiser — better —
'Till life's dream itself is past.

John Boyle O'Reilly

To _____

'Tis sweet to ride our fleet-winged ship,
As bird-like she skims away,
Before the wind, all her sails adrip,
With rainbow tinted spray.

And sweet it is in the calm to rest;
To gaze on the depths of blue;
To feel the swell of its heaving breast;
And to watch each varying hue,

That deepens, and fades, and faints away; —
   As the sun to his azure bed
Sinks slowly seeming with magic ray
   Both ocean and sky to wed

Around him is spread a nuptial veil
   Of varying colors blent.
Turning his golden beams more pale,
   As they dart through each gauzy rent,

But sweeter, beloved, to think of thee,
   Thou soul of my sweetest hours;
The memory brightens sun, sky, and sea:
   — Less bright than this love of ours.

Binn Eider. John Flood [signature]

24th (Sunday) A gorgeous sunrise this morning — The prettiest yet — we passed the Tropic of Capricorn at 8 o.c. last Evg — I've had Mass Celebrated to-day — I received Holy Communion — Our water supply reduced to-day from 14 to 7 pints — I felt quite happy to-day, as I always do when I approach the Holy Sacrament

25th — Ship going about 8 knots — rather gloomy Day — 12 o.c. S. Latitude, 28° 5', W. Long. 27° 0' — Concert as usual last night — Joe & I manage the duets capitally

26th — A gloomy day — ship doing about 6 knots — A sail in sight — 12 o.c. 30° 20' S — 24° 5' W. Long — a drizzling rain — no comfort on deck 6 o.c. going 12 Knots

27th — Running 10 Knots under square yards — thank goodness the great heat has left us — Clorid of Zinc sprinkled between decks — 12 o.c. S. Lat 32° 29' — 22°36' W. Long — Bradley struck up (immediately after dinner) 'We'll meet again together' a splendid chorus — B. is a card — I trust the song will be fulfilled & that we will be home again — however — begone dull care — I'll endeavour to drown thought by weaving a wreath of Shamrocks for next week's Goose

28th A sail in sight — a few 'Albatross's' flying about — they are very large & majestic birds — Ship going about 10 knots, S lat 32° 01' — 19° 11' West sailed 176 miles since yesterday — music on deck etc

29th — a calm beautiful morning — a beautiful sky — a sail in sight — right ahead S'Lat 34° 4' — W.Lon 19° 33' — 66 miles for the past 24 hours — a large 'Albatross' floated quite close 5 or 6 shots from a revolver fired at him — pretty good firing, but the bird escaped — I am just about preparing tonight's programme — so here goes

30th Novr — a cloudy day — 4th Copy of 'Goose' out today — the paper is improving each week — S lat 33° 54' — W. long 17° 46' — sailed 103 miles since yesterday, a nice calm Evg — Our quire hard at work practicing for tomorrow

A Mother's Love

Oh! shield her well from every pain,
Her lightest wish obey;
Thou'lt never know such love again
When she has passed away.
God round her heart that fondness tied
No human power can move;
All earthly bonds are weak beside
A mother's lasting love.

Its priceless worth thou canst not tell;
Its bonds thou canst not trace;
'Tis like the mighty ocean's swell, —
'Tis deep as endless space.
Its holy power will conquer death:
She'll watch thee from above;
Her spirit pure will guard thy path
With all her mother's love.

Time cannot break the sacred chain,
But adds a strengthening link;
Nor can the ingrate's sharpest pain
Those tender feelings sink.

Ah! no! that bond round every chord
  Thy infant fingers wove;
Thy mother's heart is always stored
  With deep undying love.

Then shield her well from every blast, —
  Let grief not mark her brow;
Nor sorrow's clouds her heart o'ercast, —
  Her days are numbered now.
A source of peace such tender care
  To thee will always prove.
Her blessing rich — her dying prayer,
  Will seal thy mother's love.

         John Boyle O'Reilly

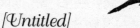

[Untitled]

In the rose-scented breeze, at the setting of sun,
In some valley's green bosom, where silver streams run,
Anacreon, when merry with wine, loved to praise
The juice of the grape in harmonious lays.

When Chian and Samian sparkled and gleamed
In goblets of gold, the poet ne'er dreamed
That in ages to come man could make merry
On drink made from beets, jocosely called sherry.

From the world of the spirits, if hither he flew,
In quest of some nectar or pure 'mountain-dew,'
Should he take what's imbibed by the staff of the 'Goose'
He'd speed back again with all haste to the deuce!

        Laoi [Edward Kelly]

1st Dec^r (Sunday) — A cloudy day — a large shoal of 'finbacks' around the ship — they can be seen feet under the water chasing each other & going at an incredible speed thro' the water. — it is a very large fish — Mass has been celebrated — Our Quire performed, we sang a beautiful <u>Kyrie</u>, Father Delany preached very fine sermon on 'Eternity.' 12 o.c. S lat 35° 15° W. Long, 143 miles

2nd — A beautiful sunrise — We expect to sight Tristan d'Acunha, and Island in the South Atlantic 1700 miles from the Cape — chain cable taken from the lockers — & Anchors got ready — as we expected to land for fresh provisions — 12 o.c., S. Lat 36° 14' W long 11° 40' — 102 miles — rather wild evening — Anchors stowed away — breeze too good to loose time.

3rd We now have droves of Cape Pigeons flying around ship — a sign (I believe) that land must be close, somewhere, this is a very wild day the waves are dashing thro the portholes & along her decks 12 o.c. S. lat 38° 03' — W. long 7° — 6 1/2' — 234 miles, numbers of 'Albatross's' flying around ship they measure 10 or 12 feet from the tip of one wing to the other.

4th Ship running at 8 Knots No 7 Mess has just been bro't before Surgeon Superintendent for the possessing of a rope — the property of Boatswain [,] Foley confined in Pepper Box — wine stopped from the rest — 12 S. lat 40° — W. long 5° — 145 miles — I was allowed on deck till 7.30 last Evg — & will enjoy this privilege till the end of the voyage — Staff of 'Goose' all allowed — I had a splendid walk & talk with Jack & John

5th — dark & foggy morning — no sailing — 12 o.c. S. lat 40° 53' W. long 3° 46' — 65 miles — No 1 Mess sang 'Well [We'll?] meet again together in our own beloved homes' After dinner beautifully.

6th — The Southern Cross can be seen nightly — I haven't had a chance to see it yet — Pompey got chain's on to-day — rainy weather 12 o.c. S. lat [no data] W. long [no data] — I have been hard at work all day for 'Goose' its to be out tomorrow

7th — A wild morning — it is believed that we may see icebergs hereabouts — 5th Copy of the 'Goose' out to-day — the leaders 'Little Things' and 'Past, Present & Future' ably written 'Live it down' dedicated to Jack by J.F., also 'Friendship' by myself for him — (see last of notes for these) — 12 o.c. S. lat 40° 50' E. long 2' — sailed 99 miles — we passed the first meridian 11 o.c. today. Our Quire is going to work — so here goes.

Live it down

When in life's battle onward fighting,
Struggling bravely day and night,
One only ray your rough path lighting —
Inward consciousness of right.
Be true and trustful — never falter —
Even though Fate may seem to frown;
Your purpose let her frown not alter:
Courage brother! Live it down.

Should calumny's sharp tongue assail you
Breathing venom — undismayed,
Let not heart nor courage fail you,
At its hiss be not afraid,
When Cynic Envy, Coward Sneering,
Would the voice of conscience drown,
Still on — unswerving and unfearing:
Courage brother! Live it down.

Still forward — calm and self-reliant,
Disdainful of the little mind;
Of scoffing ignorance defiant,
Aside not looking nor behind.
Still persevere in right for ever;
Perseverance wins the crown.
Right ever conquers — wrong will never;
Courage brother! Live it down.

Binn Éider (J.Flood [signature])

Prison Thoughts — II

Next memory turns to face Columbian shore,
　　And conjures up the blissful hours spent there
'Mongst cherished friends whom I may meet no more;
　　But Hope, soft whispering, bids me not despair.

And thou, dear friend, whose genial nature drew
　　All hearts to thee in friendship's flowery bonds,
Art ever near, and still, in fancy's view,
　　Thy willing smile to my fond wish responds.

How sweet upon our prospects to converse,
　　And proudly prophesy for each success!
We, light and careless, thought not on reverse,
　　But fondly dreamed of love and happiness.
Foul Discord through the land dissention sowed,
　　And bloody war spread horror far and wide;
And he pursued the path that duty showed,
　　And fought and bled and for his Country died.

Sleep, soldier of the North, and take thy rest,
　　Thy tombstone wreathed with glory's laurel crown,
Thy sword in honor laid across thy breast,
　　Unheeding the false world's cold smile or frown.

Soft spirit's whispers fall upon my ear
　　By orange-scented gales borne o'er the foam:
Thy friend in glory lives, be of good cheer!
　　Thou yet should meet him in a happier home.

Laoi [Edward Kelly]

Memory

I love in memory to scroll those days of peace and joy,
To blot out worldly wiles and cares, and feel again a boy;
To play along the Boyne's green banks, or through the wildwood roam;
To paint in fancy's eye once more my dear old childhood home.
Ah time! thy hand may sear the face and sow the wintry hair;
But from my heart those tender thoughts thou shalt not — cans't
      not — tear.
Though far removed from that dear spirit, yet still I love to trace
The river winding through the vale, — each bright young school
      mate's face.
To roam bird-nesting far from home, — to hear the noisy mill —
Yes, all are dear! but one loved thought is brighter, dearer still.
'Twas down beside the Boyne's green banks, beneath the leafy shade,
I told my boyish love-tale to a little brown-haired maid.
'Twas there I heard the whispered words that filled my soul with bliss,
And planted first on Mary's lips a lingering lover's kiss.
— All past and gone those dreams of joy! all fled and nought
      remained!
But memory's potent spell recalls their pleasures and their [pains?]
I pray that God may guide thy steps, and help thee, Mary, dear;
I'll never see thee more; but yet I know thou'll drop a tear
For him who loved thee first of all — who first thy lips impressed,
And told thee how he loved thee, with thy cheek upon his breast.
Oh, Memory! blest gift of God, continue still to pour
Thy softening influence on my heart till this short life is o'er.
Some crush thy spells, because thy joys may leave a trace of pain —
But wisdom — purest brightest gem — we oft through sorrow gain.

John Boyle O'Reilly

Friendship

When bleak misfortune's frown I feel,
And painful thoughts my brain oppress,
'Tis then in friendship's sweet appeal
I find relief for lost caress.

Of loving wife, whose soothings tender
So oft my weary spirits cheered,
Or lisping child, whose laugh would render
A blissful balm when grief appeared.

Though far away from my heart's treasure, —
Far, far, from all on earth I love, —
I find in friendship's hand a pressure
That cheers my path where'er I rove.
Oft pausing, when the deck I pace,
Strange forms I see around me thronging;
No genial smile lights up a face
To greet me: then with ardent longing

For sympathetic friend I sigh, —
For one whose words my heart would brighten,
To whom I'd talk of days gone by,
And try my bosom's load to lighten.

Again I'd look with anxious glancing,
And seek one friend amongst them all:
Ah, now a dear friend is advancing, —
He saw and understood the call.

Oh, Friendship! thou'rt a priceless gem; —
Aye! dearer far than brightest gold:
Thy rays can glad the heart of him
Whom worldly riches ne'er consoled.

Suir [Denis B. Cashman]

8th Wind blew great guns last night (Sunday) a wild morning — Main top-sail & a jib burst last night — no Mass — we had a sermon after which we sang the 'Litany' 12 o.c. S. lat. 40° 52' E. long. 1° 4' — 47 miles — A sail in sight on our lee — An additional blanket has just been served out to each man the weather being intensely cold — We have signalled the stranger — she is bound to Red Sea with coal

9th Dec[r] — A calm morning, ship scarcely doing 3 Knots under full canvas — 12 o.c. 40° 16' E. long 2° 10' — 63 miles — A large Albatross has been captured to-day by means of a line with bait thrown over the stern — the bird measured 10 feet from wing to wing — it has a curious bill — very long & eagle shaped at extremity — a sail in sight about ten miles off — No 5 mess drew for a Dinner — A Concert this Evg

10th — a mild morning — ship going 6 Knots — brought my bed on deck for airing — 12 o.c. S. lat 41° 6' E. Long 5° 61' — 175 miles I am in expectation of a pretty sunset

11th — fore stern sail boom sprung this morning caused by pressure of wind on sail — Cold morning — 12 o.c. 42° 21' E. long 10° 19' — 213 miles Old Joe & I are practicing some new songs — he sings nicely

12th — 12 o.c. S. lat. 43 36' E. long 15 17' — 230 miles — splendid sailing — awful cold

13th — 12 o.c. S. lat 44° 51' E. long 20° 4' — 220 miles — cold increasing — passed the longitude of the Cape at 12 o.c. last night — we were looking out for the Dutchman — no chance — so Jack had to make one — hard at work for tomorrows 'Goose'

14th — an exceedingly cold & dreary day — 12 o.c. S. lat 46° 25' E. long 24° — 206 miles — 6th copy of the 'Goose' out today — it has got better each week since its appearance — large numbers of 'Albatross's' about — a watch posted on the Forecastle Deck to look out for Icebergs in consequence of the fog — I am going to get the Quire together to practice for tomorrow

Erring Ones

What power, next the holy word which God to man has given,
Can guide the wayward heart from sin and lead the way to
heaven?
Or when the soul is deeply plunged in Error's scathing flood,
What holy feeling still remains to lure it back to good?
What it is — even [Crimes?] with shame can drive it not away
'Tis the memory and the love of her who taught us how to pray.
Oh! tis powerful and holy — he who feels it is not lost —
Tho' darkening be the sea on which his wayward soul is tossed.
He who still looks back to childhood — still her loving face recalls —
On whose ear again in memory her gentle warning falls,
Whose heart those tender thoughts enshrine — tho' of all else bereft —
And harsh to outward eye — has something good and noble left.
Where'er his mother's spirit is, a suppliant voice is there,
And God will hear before all else a mother's earnest prayer.
But some there are — alas! not few — the erring path have trod,
For whom no mother's voice is raised to plead their cause with God;
No gentle warning voice is there, nor tender thoughts can come;
They have no fond remembrances of childhood or of home.
In want — and vice — uncared for — thro' life they wander on;
God help them! they have nothing [when?] thy holy grace is gone.
Oh, judge them not too harshly, ye who dwell in happier spheres:
Were your spirits, think you, spotless, had your lot been like to
theirs?
Help them, cheer them, and with words supply another's place;
'Tis the truest act of Christian love to win them back to grace.
Think of Him who came to earth to call the sinners from their way;
Help the erring ones — His children — and thou shalt not pass away:
He who e'en 'a cup of water' to His little ones has given
Shall be paid by endless treasure and eternal rest in Heaven.

John Boyle O'Reilly

Louisa Hayden

Oh, once I loved a maiden
Darling sweet Louisa Hayden,
And my lip was honey laden
     And as happy as a dream

Her sweet laugh, like music ringing,
Her light step, elastic springing
And a thousand loves were winging
     From her glance's ardent beam.

E'en the memory of her glances
Yet like mystic spell entrances,
Spite of time that still advances
     Swiftly blotting o'er life's chart.

But how e'er he may endeavour
To efface it, he can never
The sweet maiden's image sever
     From its altar in my heart.

Fresh as moss-rose in a bower,
When the dew a diamond shower
Falling bright on leaf and flower
     Breathing perfumes in the air

Like a dewy moss-rose glowing
Heart and eyes with love oerflowing
And a perfume ever blowing
     From her waving golden hair

Oh, how sweet was every meeting
When I heard her loving greeting,
Alas! Alas! too fleeting
      Was that bright ecstatic time,

When she my life was blessing,
Pure and trustful and caressing,
With a blush her love confessing
      In love's willing pantomine [sic].

'Neath bowers of jasmine smiling,
Like the flow'rs our souls entwining,
As we watched our star outshining
      Souls as thrilling as its beam.

Oh! how I loved that maiden,
Darling sweet Louisa Hayden,
In those days of bliss oerladen
      When my life was like a dream.

                              Binn Éider [John Flood]

The Old School Clock

Old memories rush oer my mind just now
Of faces and friends of the past,
Of that happy time when life's dream was all bright,
E'er the clear sky of youth was o'ercast.

Very dear are those mem'ries, — they've clung round my heart,
And bravely withstood times rude shock;
But not one is more hallowed or dear to me now
Than the face of the Old School Clock.

'Twas a quaint old clock, with a quaint old face,
And great iron weights and chains;
It stopped when it liked, — and before it struck,
It creaked as if twere in pain,

It had seen many years, and it seemed to say,
'I'm one of the real old stock,'
To the youthful fry, who with reverence looked
On the face of the Old School Clock.

How many a time have I labored to sketch
That yellow and time-honored face,
With its basket of flowers, its figures and hands,
And the weights and chains in their place!

How oft have I gazed with admiring eye
As I sat on the wooden block,
And pondered and guessed at the wonderful things
That were inside that Old School Clock!

What a terrible frown did the Old Clock wear
To the truant who timidly cast
An anxious eye on those merciless hands
Which for him had been moving too fast!

But it lingered not long, for it loved to smile
On that noisy thoughtless flock,
And it creaked and whirred and struck with glee, —
Did that genial, good-humoured Old Clock.

Well, years had passed, and my mind was filled
With the world's cares and ways,
When again I stood in that little school
Where I passed my boy hood's days.

My old friend was gone! and there hung a thing
Which my sorrow seemed to mock,
As I gazed with a throbbing and softened heart
On a new fashioned German clock.

'Twas a gaudy thing with bright-painted sides,
And it looked with an insolent stare
On the desks and the seats and on everything old
And I thought of the friendly air —

Of the face that I missed, with its weights and chains —
All gone to the Auctioneer's block:
'Tis a thing of the past, — I never more shall see
But in mem'ry that Old School Clock.

'Tis the way of the world — old friends pass away,
And fresh faces arise in their stead;
But still 'mid the din and the bustle of life,
We cherish fond thoughts of the dead.

Yes, dear are those mem'ries — they've clung round my heart
And bravely withstood time's rude shock;
But not one is more hallowed or dear to me now
Than the face of that Old School Clock.

JBO'Reilly [signature]

15th (Sunday) — A very cold day — the ship's bell is tolling for Catholic service (first time) no mass — we had communion & sang Litany & Tantum — 12 o.c. 47° 5' E. long 28° 29' — 216 miles since yesterday — no concert

16th — a rough morning — 12 o.c. S. lat 48° 8' 34° 2' E. long — 231 miles — a Convict named Thomas Corcoran died at 6.15 AM this morning — I saw the poor fellow smoking on the hatch a few days since — He is to be buried this Evg. at 6 o.c. p.m. — Ship running 10 Knots — 3 o.c. p.m. — at 5.45 all hands collected on the Forecastle — where the body (sewed up in canvas) lay stretched, on a grating — I for the first time witnessed the melancholy sight of a funeral at Sea — the Convicts ranged themselves at either side of the starboard side of the ship — & on the forecastle Deck — & after a few minutes the procession began — a cross bearer leading — he was followed by two acolites followed by an Officiating Priest in robes — & his clerk — next came the Corpse covered with the Union Jack borne by 6 Convicts — when the procession reached the inside of the bulkhead door 'The Misereri' and 'Te Deum' were repeated — the body being placed in a slanting position projecting from a Starboard porthole — at the conclusion of the prayers the body with a heavy weight tied to the feet, was gradually allowed to slip — a splash immediately intimated that it was consigned to its watery grave — the whole scene was very solemn and impressive — I hope he may requiescat in pace — the Priest says the poor fellow died a good Christian.

17th Dec^r — Jack and I had a long chat in bed last night on yesterdays funeral — a large 'Albatross' has just alighted on the ships boats that swings from Davits — fired at —

not hit — 12 o.c. 48° 18' E. long 39° 29' — very cold — 207 miles — flocks of Cape Pigeons & Albatrosses flying about

18th Dec^r — glass at 41 in the shade — awful cold — 12 o.c. 48° 49' E. long 44° 44' — sailed 210 miles — I am up to my eyes in papers to-day — weaving wreaths of holly & ivy, and shamrocks for the Christmas N° of 'The Wild Goose' I expect it will look very pretty — Practicing the 'Adesti' this Evg for mass — I expect to do it well

19th — on Deck early — wild morning — Thermometer very low — cold intense — 12 o.c. S. lat 49° 8' E. long 49° 25' — 185 miles — a chain & rope fell from fore top-sail this morning — no one hit — I have just finished the headings — Jack says its beautiful executed, I believe he has good taste

20th. — Jack & I slept till breakfast served — I got a supply of 4 sticks of tobacco to-day, 12 o.c. S. lat 48° 45' E. long 54° 48' — sailed 215 miles since yesterday — Our last number of the 'Goose' to appear on tomorrow, it will be double the usual size — some beautiful poems are to appear — Our quire are hard at work for xmas

21st — Ship running at 7 Knots under full Canvas — 12
o.c. S. lat 48° 37' E. long 58° 54' — 162 miles — Our
Christmas Goose out to-day — it is the best number yet —
its Contents are — a pretty heading 'Adieu' a beautiful
article by J.F. — 'Farewell' another by Jack — 'Norah
Daly' a tale by Kelly — 'Future' by Father D — Poems
'The Flying Dutchman' by Jack — 'Cremona' a poem —
one of the battles of 'The Wild Geese' (the Brigade) —
'Christmas Night' a poem by Jack — [squiggle for 'etc.']

22nd We are all wishing most anxiously for the termination
of the voyage — great preparations for xmas — each mess
saving flour & fruit — (Sunday) Mass on board — Quire
sang — very cold day — 12 o.c. S. lat 49° 15' E. long 62°
44' — 156 miles — this is the coldest day we have had yet
— it's miserable on deck

23rd — very cold — 12 o.c. S. lat 47° 58' E. l 67° 38' —
219 miles since yesterday — 4 o.c. PM 2 whales seen,
spouting water 60 feet high

24th (Christmas Eve) a fine morning — Sea of beautiful
green color — droves of 'Albatrosses' flying about — two
captured — very cold — 12 o.c. S. lat 46° 52' E. long 71°
39' — 175 miles — we expect a gale to night — sky looks
threatening — All hands practicing the 'Adesti' for
tomorrow — I prayed for the Dear ones at home very
fervently to night — may God grant them a happy xmas

25th <u>Christmas Day</u> — Before I arose this morning the 'Adesti' was sung by all hands — some dressed, others in their bunks — I immediately dressed — went on Deck — had a fresh water wash — We had a terrible storm last night, which has not yet abated, the ship is being tossed about like old boots — & shipping heavy seas — we have just breakfasted off a Sweet loaf (rather a delicacy to Convicts) and have another for Skilly 12 o.c. No mass, ship too unsteady — Communion administered — We sang in admirable style — J.F. and I had a chat about home — 1 o.c. we have just dined off plum duff & salt horse, rather venerable — wine served at 2 o.c. 2 glasses to each — after which I had a smoke & went below to hear our Christmas Goose read by Jack — I feel rather cheerful today, thank God — I sincerely trust that my dear K, Anne, Billy & our dear boys are enjoying a happy Xmass — I feel the day is not so far distant when I shall again press them to my bosom, which is all the happiness I care for, in this world, and even in a strange far off country I can be happy — these dear ones can make me inexpressably happy in any country — God bless them, I waft them my blessings & a 1000 kisses across the 1000^{s} of miles which divide us — 12 o.c. S. lat 46° 2' E. long 74° 12' — 117 miles since yesterday — no Skilly — very rough all day & a nasty night anticipated

Cinderella

More graceful than the bounding Fawn,
    More loving than the dove,
More fresh and bright than morning's dawn,
    Art thou my treasured love.
No wealth is thine, no courtly grace,
    To dazzle with their glare,
But heaven is breathing from thy face
    And on thy golden hair.

Agra machree! my darling one!
    The love I bear for thee
More fervid is than summer sun,
    And deeper than the sea:
And deeper in my soul it [grows?]
    With every passing breath,
The life pulse of my heart it flows
    To cease alone in death.

What destiny is thine, Asthore!
    Disdain — Contumely:
The fair sweet girl of fairy lore
    Less hapless seems than thee:
'Tis crime to love thee — darkest crime
    'Gainst those who hate thee so;
Thy sisters' envy grows with time
    As hers did long ago.

I would have dried thy tearful eyes
    And shielded thee from scorn;
And won thee honor's brightest prize
    Thy beauty to adorn:

For this I braved the frown of hate,
The law's harsh dark decree;
Mavrone! Thine is a bitter fate —
A felon's doom for me.

I still unceasing pray for thee
To the Almighty Throne, —
Pray that I once again may see
My darling one, my own, —
To see her once before I die;
Oh, sweet would be my rest,
Could I but breathe my latest sigh
Upon my darling's breast.

Binn Éider [John Flood]

Christmas Garland

Come, banish care and dull despair;
'Tis Merry Christmas time;
Then close around, and hear resound
A story told in rhyme.
A Christmas story, of fame and glory,
That ne'er will fade, of 'The Brigade.'
For us, to-night, 'twill sound as bright
As merry Christmas chime.

And when 'tis told, we will unfold
An ocean legend true,
Of dreadful spell that erst befell
'The Dutchman' and his crew.

No Christmas tree grows on the sea
No berries bright, of red or white,
And ill retrieves their loss, the 'leaves'
    Around we strew.

But ever still, through good or ill,
    We welcome Christmas Day.
No loved ones near, nor cup to cheer,
    And brighten up our way;
Yet banish care and dull despair,
For Christmas cheer we'll each draw near,
And let to-night, our hearts grow bright,
    In friendship's ray.

John Flood

Cremona

All dark and sullen was the night, and red the sun went down
Behind the towers and battlements of old Cremona town
Sullen the blustering March wind swept the waters of the Po
Trench, ravelin, and parallel of France's baffled foe —
Austria's legions and their chief, the gallant Prince Eugene,
Who tried for months the town to take by storm but tried in vain;
Upon its walls the fleur-de-lis still waved in haughty joy
Above the brave defenders and their Marshal Villeroy —
Waved o'er the the Sons of Sunny France, her bravest and her best —
Waved oer the men of the 'Brigade' — the Wild Geese of the West,
Full oft the walls high o'er the fight, had rung with Irish cheers,
As fiercely on the foe dashed Burke's and Dillons Grenadiers —

For ever where in fiercest fight her banner France unrolled
Her Irish Allies still were found the bravest to uphold
Her honor and on many a field, in many a bloody fray,
Those foster-Sons of France have turned the fortunes of the day,
Nor grudged to their adopted land their dead so thickly strewn
But fiercely dealt her vengeance out, whilst waiting for their own
— 'Tis night within Cremona's walls, all silent as the dead
Nought heard is but the plashing rain, the Sentry's measured tread
Is muffled by the gusty wind, in eddying blasts that sweep,
All else is hushed, the garrison is weary and asleep:
Divided by the river Po, their force lay thus arrayed —
The southern town held by the French, the north by the Brigade.
A narrow bridge connects the town, and whilst their comrades
     slept
By thirty-seven of the Gael a watchful eye is kept —
And many a heart is winging back away across the main
To that dear land they loved so well, but ne'er may see again,
They dream of homes by Shannon's side where they so often
     played
Bright happy careless boys, before they donned the white cockade,
Of heart-loved scenes that smiling lie by Leinster's vales and rills,
By Ulster's glens, and Connaught's plains, and Munster's lakes
     and hills.
They dream of friendship and of love — they dream of bliss and
     woe
Of Glory's fields where the 'Brigade' was charging on the foe.
But dream not that, by traitor led, the Austrians now creep
With bated breath and stealthy step upon them while they sleep.
The sentry, too, is musing, as before the northern gate,
With measured step and piercing eye, and hero heart elate,
He paces through the rain and gloom, but on the muttering blast
Hears not the foe whose serried ranks are gathering thick and fast.
A curse upon the traitor wretch, who to the wily foe
For sordid gold the town betrayed! A sewer that ran below

The walls — its bed had long been dried, and save to him alone
It hidden lay, unusèd, unsuspected, and unknown —
Thro' this he led the Austrians and now thick thro' the night
Their columns sudden break upon the startled sentry's sight.
His warning cry rings up into the very vault of heaven,
As rush the legions of Eugene around the Thirty Seven,
And ere his cry had died away, their Irish bullets tore
A yawning gap right through their ranks — their steel was red with
      gore
As with one cry — as when in wrath the lion from his lair
Enragèd springs — they slash upon the foeman's closing square;
Again, and still again they charge with cheers upon their ranks.
But columns massing denser still are closing on their flanks.
Then inch by inch, before the foe, outnumbered back they fell
Yet high above their muskets' peal uprose their maddened yell
As fast they fired, reloaded, and then fired and charged again
Marking the bloody way they went with heaps of foemen slain.
Their numbers now are thinning fast, but still they bravely fight,
As wolf dog 'gainst the howling wolves defends the flock at night
Their cry grows weaker as they fall, and all are bleeding fast,
When to their ears a thrilling shout comes ringing on the blast,
And in their shirts rush thro' the night — a tempest on the sea —
Their comrades of the 'Old Brigade' led by O'Mahony. —
When in the night the fierce typhoon sweeps white upon a fleet
That turns and flies before its screams, afraid its wrath to meet;
So in their shirts those grenadiers rushed screaming thro' the blast
Upon the panic stricken foe that fled before them fast.
Back, back they drove, before their wrath, a struggling, shattered
      wreck
And vainly strove with hurried fire that hurricane to check;
But fast the foe came pouring in. Eugene in the town hall
Commands, and thirty thousand men are rushing to his call.
But numbers heed not the Brigade, as like avenging fates
In that fierce Irish tempest rush, they drive them to the gates.

There, cheering high above the fight, outnumbered ten to one,
They hand to hand still held their own, still gallantly fought on —
They fought, like tigers for their young, as oft they fought before,
But higher into Glory's skies did 'Wild Geese' never soar.
God's blessing fall upon their names, their race, and on their land!
Where'er they strike, may heaven guide, and strengthen still each
      hand —
Still hand to hand they fiercely fought, and steel and bullet sped,
Bright deeds of valor doing 'till their shirts with blood were red;
But fast they're falling — faster — as the bullets shower like rain
Now thro' the gates the Austrians are surging back again;
Before their massing columns they retired, but did not yield
But turn at bay and charged them back until their column reeled.
Back step by step, across the bridge, with care already mined,
With serried ranks they face the foe, and blow it up behind.
But now the French rush to their aid — they hear their rapid tramp;
Again they cheer and charge the foe and drive them to their camp —
Bright deeds of chivalry were done that night by the 'Brigade';
But with the Austrians fought one whose name will never fade.
McDowell! he was Irish, too! We hail his name with joy,
Who charged that night thro' thickest fight, and captured Villeroy.
He scorned the bribe to set him free — Yet higher grows his fame!
A soldier still to honor true, and to his Irish name —
The morning broke, and in the air the Oriflamme still waved
Proud over Old Cremona's walls — by Irish valor saved;
But dear they bought that victory — those sons of Innisfail,
And while *Te Deum* swells in France for victory — a wail.
Went up to heaven from their own land — a death wail for her
      brave
Who fell beneath a foreign flag, so far beyond the wave,
And with the wail of agony, a fervent prayer arose
To Heaven for one such victory at home oer Ireland's foes.

                           Binn Éider [John Flood]

The Flying Dutchman

Long, long ago, from Amsterdam, a vessel sailed away,
As fair a ship as ever rode amidst the dashing spray;
Fond loving hearts were on the shore, and scarfs were in the air
As to her o'er the Zuyder Zee they waft adieu and prayer.
Her gaudy pennant streamed aloft, and as she skimmed the seas,
Each taper mast was bending like a rod before the breeze.
Within her there were gallant hearts, tho' filled with sadness now,
For still the lingering kiss was fresh on lip and brow.
Her captain was a stalwart man — an iron heart had he;
From childhood's days he sailed upon the rolling Xuyder Zee.
He nothing feared upon the earth, nor scarcely Heaven feared,
He would have dared and done whatever mortal man had dared[.]
He turned him from the swelling sail and gazed upon the shore
Ah! little thought the skipper those 'twould meet his eye no more.
He dreamt not that an awful doom was hanging on his ship, —
That Vanderdecken's name would yet make pale the speaker's lip[.]
The revel bounded on her way, and spire and dome went down:
Ere darkness fell, beneath the wave had sunk the distant town.
No more, no more, ye hapless crew, shall Holland meet your eye
As lingering hope and keen suspense [in?] maid, wife, and child
     shall die.
Away, away the vessel speeds, — but sea and sky alone
Is round her as her course she steers across the torrid zone.
Away, away! The north star fades, the southern cross is high,
And myriad stars of brightest beam are sparkling in the sky.
The tropic winds are left behind — she nears the Cape of Storms,
There awful Tempest sits enthroned in wild and dread alarms:

Where Ocean in his fury heaves aloft his foaming crest,
And dashes round the helpless ship that rides upon his breast.
Fierce raged the mountain billows round the Dutchman's gallant
   craft,
But Vanderdecken to their rage a loud defiance laughed.
Tho' wave and tempest barred his way, he braved them in his
   pride,
As onward still his Course he held, and wind and wave defied.
He struggled madly forward in the weird unearthly fight;
His brow was black, his eye was fierce; but looks of wild afright
Were passed amongst the silent crew as still they onward steered:
They did not dare to question, but they whispered what they feared.
They knew their black-browed captain — 'neath his darkened eye
   they quailed
And in a grim and sullen mood their bitter fate bewailed.
He never swerved, but day and night the deck he sternly paced,
As 'fore the hurricane the ship like some fleet courser raced.
He fought the tempest inch by inch, and conquered — so he
   thought —
But ah! he little dreamed how dear that victory was bought.
Again his loud defiant laugh he shouted to the blast —
The placid ocean smiled beyond — the dreaded Cape was passed.
Away across the Indian main the gallant vessel glides,
And gentle murmuring ripples break along her graceful sides.
The perfumed breezes waft her on — her destined port she nears:
The Dutchman's brow has lost its frown — the mariners their fears.
'Land ho!' at length the welcome sound the watchful sailor sings,
And soon within an Indian bay the ship at anchor swings.
Not idle then the busy crew — ere long the spacious hold
Is emptied of its western freight, and stored with India's gold.
Again the ponderous Anchor's weighed — the shore is left behind,
The snowy sails are bosomed out before the favouring wind,
The [——] deep around her seems a calm and mirrored lake,
And [——] trains of sparkling light are gleaming in her wake.

For Home she steers! She seems to know and answer to the word,
And swifter skims the burnished deep like some fair ocean bird.
'For home! for home!' The joyous crew, with gladsome voices cry,
And e'en the dark-browed skipper has a mild light in his eye;
He looks above, where streaming high, the pennant cuts the blue,
And every rope, and spar, and sail is firm, and strong, and true.
He pictures to himself the day when once again he'll see
The spires and domes of Amsterdam rise o'er the Zuyder Zee.
Away across the burning zone the vessel southward flies,
Again the northern beacons fade and southern stars arise.
Oh! hapless crew, you little dream, as onward still you go,
That o'er your fair ill-fated ship is hung a doom of woe.
Again the stormy cape draws near, and furious billows rise
And once again the Dutchman's laugh both wind and wave
        defies.
But fiercely swept the tempest ere the scornful laugh had died,
A warning to the daring man to curb his impious pride.
A crested mountain struck the ship, and like a frightened bird
She trembled 'neath the awful shock, — then Vanderdecken heard
A pleading voice within the gale — his better angel spoke,
But fled before his scowling look; then fierce the billows broke
Upon the trembling helpless ship — the crew with terror paled,
But still the captain never flinched, nor 'neath their fury quailed.
With arms folded o'er his breast, and fiercely flashing eye,
He answered back the angry frown that lowered o'er the sky.
He seized the helm in his grasp, and fiercely dashed aside
The trembling wretch who had held it, then with heart of scornful
        pride,
All heedless of the warning blast or lightning's lurid [flame?],
He spoke — and thus with impious words blasphemed God's holy
        name.
'Howl on, ye winds! ye tempests, howl! your rage is spent in vain;
Despite your strength, your frowns, your hate, I'll ride upon the
        main,

117

Dash on, ye waves! across your foam I'll sail my path:
I care not for thy Maker's smile — I care not for His wrath!"
He ceased — a deathlike silence reigned — the tempest and the sea
Were hushed in sudden stillness by their Ruler's dread decree.
All motionless the vessel rode within the gathering gloom;
The Dutchman stood upon the poop and heard his awful doom;
The mariners were on the deck, in swooning terror prone;
Their heart's blood froze — they, too, were doomed; in angered
*   mighty tone*
The awful words swept o'er the deep — 'Go, wretch! accursed!
*   condemned!*
Go sail forever on the deep, by angry tempests hemmed!
No home, no port, no calm, no rest, no gentle fav'ring breeze,
Shall ever greet thee. Go, accursed! and battle with the seas.
Go, braggart! struggle with the storm, nor ever cease to live,
But bear a million times the pangs that death and fear can give.
Away, and hide that guilty head! a curse to all thy kind
Who ever see thee struggling, wretch! with ocean and with wind.
Away, presumptuous worm of earth! Go teach thy fellow worms,
The awful doom that waits on him who braves the King of
*   Storms!"*
'Twas o'er! One lurid gleam of wrath lit up the sea and sky
Around and o'er the fated ship: There rose a wailing cry
From every heart within her of wild anguish and despair;
But mercy was for them no more — it died away in air.
Again the lurid light gleamed out — the ship was still at rest,
The crew were standing at their posts: with arms across his breast
Still stood the captain on the poop — but bent and crouching now
He bowed before that <u>fiat</u> dread, and o'er his swarthy brow
Came lines of anguish as if he a thousand years of pain
Had lived and suffered — then across the heaving angry main
The tempest shrieked triumphant, and the waves in madness
*   dashed*
And hissed their scorn o'er the ship round which their fury crashed.

And ever, ever, ever thus, that doomed crew will speed,
They try to round the stormy cape, but never will succeed.
And oft when storms are fiercest, 'mid the lightning's vivid sheen,
Against the tempest struggling, still the phantom ship is seen
Across the billows dashing; and it's said that every word
Of her captain's awful blasphemy upon the gale is heard.
But Heaven help the hapless crew that impious sentence hears;
The doom of those is sealed to whom that fatal ship appears:
They'll never reach their destined port — they'll see their homes no
      more:
They who see the Flying Dutchman never, never reach the shore.

John Boyle O'Reilly

[Note: The two blank spaces in the poem occur in lines which were damaged in the copies of The Wild Goose *with which I was working, and which do not appear at all in the version of 'The Flying Dutchman' in Roche.]*

A Merry Christmas

A 'Merry Christmas!' each one sends
    To-night across the foam,
To all the loved ones — all the friends
    Who think of us at home.

From them a 'Merry Christmas!' flies
    On angel's pinions bright;
'Tis heard upon the breeze that sighs
    Around our ship tonight.

Though on our ears no voices fall,
　　Our hearts — our spirits hear —
'A Merry Christmas to you all —
　　And happy, bright New Year!'

Then, brothers! Though we spend the day
　　Within a prison ship,
Let every heart with hope be gay, —
　　A smile on every lip.

Let's banish sorrows — banish fears,
　　And fill our hearts with glee,
And ne'er forget in after years
　　Our Christmas on the sea.

John Boyle O'Reilly

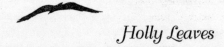

Holly Leaves

What flower so gay as the holly spray;
　　With berries so red and bright?
In the frosty rime of Christmas time,
　　Hearts gladdened are at the sight.
'Tis the rarest tree in Christandie!
　　When recalling old Christmas time,
We link the sheen of its leaves so green
　　With the merry joybells' chime.

Oh! dear to me is the holly-tree —
　　Dear the robin's carolled song,
And the mystic bough of the mistletoe,
　　That to Christmas times belong.

Fenian Diary

When the earth is white, and the sky is bright,
     On the silent frosty air,
From the holly bush, how sweet the gush
     Of the robin's song of prayer.

When with wassail bowl we cheer the soul,
     While the yule-logs cheery glow,
We kiss our girls beneath the pearls
     Of the mystic mistletoe.
When hearts are light and eyes are bright,
     And lips like berries shine,
And draughts of joy, without alloy,
     We quaff with the rich red wine.

Oh! red and white are the berries bright
     Of holly and mistletoe;
When winter's breath breathes frozen death,
     On all else — still bright they glow;
To gladden the walls of princely halls,
     And the peasant's cottage hearth,
In the happy time where the joyous chime
     Rings 'Peace to men on earth!'

No holly have we, nor revelry,
     Nor robin's song to cheer;
From the mistletoe, away we go,
     To a distant hemisphere.
Where all is strange and full of change
     But still where'er we roam,
My heart yet clings to the hallowed things
     Of Christmas time at home.

Binn Éider [John Flood]

Welcome Merry Christmas

Tune your voices full of laughter,
Dash away the dark hereafter,
Fling the cup of sorrow down, boys;
Laugh tonight at Fate's dark frown, boys;
    Banish sorrow,
    And joy borrow,
To welcome merry Christmas time.

Quaff of mirth a brimming measure, —
Mirth tonight's our only treasure,
It will warm our hearts like wine, boys;
None tonight should weep or pine, boys;
    Not with sadness,
    But with gladness,
We'll welcome merry Christmas time.

What are all life's joys and troubles?
Nought but empty fleeting bubbles;
But heaven lends a joy divine, boys,
More bright and warm than ruddy wine, boys,
    Joy that fires us,
    And inspires us,
To welcome merry Christmas time.

Binn Éider [John Flood]

Kate

I dream of thee, my bonnie Kate,
 And bow my heart,
And mourn the bitter, bitter fate
 That did us part.
As Autumn leaves when the sun is gone
 My heart is sere;
The sun of my life most brightly shone
 When thou wert near.
Dreams of thy beauty, darling Kate,
 So fresh and bright,
Come floating, and my soul elate,
 Wakes from its night.
A graceful lily in the wind,
 I see thy form;
A lily's incense is thy mind:
 [Fled?] in the storm,
With heaven's best, holiest balm
 It fills each sense, —
Like prayer, — with a holy calm, —
 Love's recompense
Dreams of thy beauty, Darling Katie,
 Thine eyes dark night —
Those orbs from which doth calmly shine
 Thy soul so bright.
Thine archèd brow, and drooping lid, —
 Where wily Love
His heart-enslaving bonds had hid, —
 Thine eyes above;

Thy pouting lips, and laughing face,
  And auburn hair,
Thy snowy neck — thy every grace
  Beyond compare —
And in my dreams thy hand I kiss,
  And search thine eyes
For the old, old look of love and bliss
  My heart's best prize.
The pressure of thy hand I feel,
  So soft and warm:
To worship that fair hand I kneel,
  My heart a storm
Of love and anguish, bliss and pain
  — For ah! I deem
I'll never press thy hand again
  Save in a dream.
I dream, my Kate, how bright thou art,
  And when I wake
The thorn is deeper in my heart
  That <u>will not</u> break.

Binn Éider [John Flood]

Christmas Night

'Twas Christmas Day, as the evening fell, and the gladsome
  sounds of mirth
O'er the City's darkening streets rang out from many a happy hearth:
The North Wind loved the joyous tones, and he whistled his
  loudest blast
Of boisterous mirth round those cheerful homes, as he rapidly
  hurried past.

Away o'er the fields and woods he rushed, but he paused in his
    wild career
For again through the gathering gloom arose, those sounds he
    loved to hear.
Then down to a cottage far below he stooped in his rapid flight, —
And he shouted with glee, did the old North Wind, on that happy
    Christmas night.
Away again o'er the woods and wilds — all wrapt in a snowy
    shroud;
But soon in the path of the old North Wind, rose a Castle's turrets
    proud;
The sound of the feast, and the song, and the dance, came cheerily
    from below,
And the great yule-log in the Castle's hall sent out its genial glow.
The Old Wind paused with a beaming smile, and peered at the
    happy throng,
Then round that noble castle's walls, he roared his boisterous song.
Oh! he loved those sounds, and he lingered awhile, to feast in the
    pleasing sight,
Then away again, with a laugh and a shout, making glad that
    Christmas night.
O'er country, and city, and hamlet he sped, and from all came
    joyous sounds,
The Old Wind whirled and shrieked with glee, for he soon would
    finish his rounds.
Away o'er the forest and field he swept, and his voice grew hoarse
    and proud,
As low to the rude Old Tyrant's power the forest monarchs bowed.
A mighty oak from its roots he tore and hurled aloft from his path:
'How strong I am,' said the Old North Wind; 'Oh! who can
    withstand my wrath?'
And thus he spoke as he onward sped — 'truly every heart is light;
In merry England from the east to the west, no mortal is sad
    tonight!'

But now in his path stood a gloomy pile, ere the cheering thought
*   had passed:*
A prison, all massive, and silent, and stern, its darké[?]ning
*   shadow cast.*
The air grew cold and his boisterous mirth was struck with a
*   sudden chill;*
For tho' keen are the frozen blasts of the North, there are others
*   more piercing still.*

Sadly he blew round the ponderous walls, for he saw not a sign of
*   mirth;*
Though he peered into every grated cell, no sound of joy came
*   forth.*
'Now,' said he, 'I must blow a cheery blast;' and he essayed a
*   merry tone;*
But he failed, and he shook his grisly locks, as it died in a hollow
*   moan.*
Then the Old Wind heaved a mighty sigh, 'Oh "woe" is me!' did he
*   say,*
'That I must return with such saddening thoughts from such a
*   cheerful day.'*
As thus he mused from a window sill, he gazed o'er the dismal
*   place;*
Then turning, he looked within the cell and beheld an upturned
*   face,*
All rigid and pale, and with lowering brow looking out on the
*   gathering night;*
The Old King gazed through the mortal's soul, and with pity was
*   moved at the sight.*

He looked in the depths of the troubled heart, and an Evil Spirit
*   was there:*
'Ah!' said he, as he gazed at the stoney eye, 'tis the work of grim
*   Despair;*

Who is seeking his prey on this blessed night, but I swear by my
    crown of snow
That I'll thwart his plan 'gainst this wretched man ere I back to my
    ice caves go!'
Then a cheering note did the Old Wind blow, as he entered the
    gloomy cell;
But all in vain were his cheering tones — still the restless footsteps
    fell.
Again he blew in a stronger Key, till at length his loudest roar
He had tried in despair; still the wretched man was heedless as
    before,
And with hasty step his dungeon paced with a fevered throbbing
    brain,
And the Spirit of Evil triumphant laughed at the Old Wind's efforts
    in vain.
But once more he paused in his weary walk to gaze with
    abstracted eye
Through the massive bars that in bold relief stood out 'gainst the
    wintry sky.
Again as the Old Wind scanned that face his courage revived; and
    now
Like Zephyr, soft as an Angel's wing, he played o'er that troubled
    brow.
He gently fanned the fevered cheek and cooled the throbbing brain,
'Till the heart grew calmer and the eye had lost its weary look of pain;
The broken spirit he mildly soothed with a low and plaintive air,
'Till at length the weary soul he lured from the grasp of dark
    Despair.
The troubled heart was now at rest, and borne on the Cadence mild.
Came long-forgotten scenes of youth, where he played a happy
    child;
But softer still the Old Wind blew, and recalled his father's death,
And his mother's voice — and a sob burst forth, for he felt her
    loving breath

Again on his brow: then he bowed his head 'neath the Father's
 chastening rod,
And the penitent tears gushed freely forth as he raised his soul to
 God.
Then as he prayed, a heavenly voice brought peace to his heaving
 breast,
Saying — 'Come to me all you weary ones, and I will give you rest.'
'Oh! how glad I am' said the Old North Wind; 'now back again
 I'll go
To my own loved north, 'mid the icebergs vast and the pure eternal
 snow.'
Ah! well might he sing his boisterous song on his rapid homeward
 flight,
For a stricken soul made its peace with God on that blessed
 Christmas night.

John Boyle O'Reilly

Christmas Eve

With holly branch, and ivy bough,
And mistletoe is gaily dight
Each homestead, and Old Christmas' brow
Is crowned with evergreen tonight, —
A snowy mantle's on the grass —
Old frozen Winter placed it there.
And trooping to the midnight mass,
Our hearts are filled with holy prayer
 To-welcome blessed Christmas.

The church is all ablaze with light,
And pious hands have placèd there
Festoons of brilliant green and white:
The Crib arrayed with holy care,
From God's high altar there ascends
A light, like glory's brightest beam;
The organ's peal, that melting blends
Our souls into a blissful dream,
      To-welcome holy Christmas.

The acolytes and priest arrayed —
The 'Gloria' breaks upon the ear
The grosser thoughts of earth then fade,
And falls a bliss from holier sphere.
Oh! there are souls so pure and bright
That hear the angel host that sings
His praise, and 'peace to men' tonight,
And hear the rustle of their wings,
      This holy blessed Christmas.

Then homeward through the frosty night,
With kindly hearts and eyes aglow;
With spirits buoyant, stepping light,
We crunch the white and frozen snow;
And hands with cordial grasp are pressed,
And laughing voices cheerful greet
Each other, and in every breast
A kindred heart doth warmly beat,
      To-wish 'a merry Christmas'

Binn Éider [John Flood]

26th the storm continues unabated — Seas are shipped every half hour — Sea running high — mountain waves — ship buried every moment & encompassed by huge seas as high as her top masts — 12 o.c. S. lat 46° 3' E. long 79° 8' — sailed 206 miles since yesterday — 5 o.c. storm abating but Sea still high — M^{c}G treated us to some plum D

27th A very fine morning — the storm which lasted since xmass Eve has entirely disappeared — We sang the Adesti after breakfast — Ship running 10 Knots under full canvas — 12 o.c. S. lat 45° 9' E. long 84° 8' — sailed 219 miles since 12 yesterday — Sun encircled with a luminous halo — the sailors say it indicates a storm — I hope not — I got a supply of tobacco to-day 12 sticks

28th We've had a rather rough night — a gale commenced 12.30 o.c. p.m. & has not yet abated — all hands are stowing away the fore-top sheet — 12 o.c. S. lat 44° 9' E. long 84° 38' — 63 miles — gale abating — 5 o.c. a calm has just set in — shipping seas

29th Morning wild — 12 o.c. S. lat 42° 38' E. lat 89° 20' — 230 miles — I received a present of a beautiful Sweet loaf which J.F., Jack, Tom & I have just discussed — and had a long chat afterwards

30th A fine day on Deck at 10 AM. — 12 o.c. S. lat 42° 1'
E. long 93° 28' — 188 miles — Old Joe & I sang 'I've
wandered in dreams' & 'Norah' in beautiful style — and
some other pretty airs — we sing well together — we gave
up just now — 8 o.c. pm — said prayers & tumbled in,
where Jack & I will talk ourselves to sleep — It blew
awfully this night — I have never heard such winds.

31st Dec[r] — Weather getting warm — on deck at 7 o.c. —
12 o.c. S. lat 40° 15' E. long 96° 30' — 174 miles since
yesterday — John F. & Jack hard at work copying our
xmas number of 'The Goose' for the Capt[n] who asked for
a copy of it. I have just dined off Salt Horse & biscuit. N°1
& My Mess (2) having saved our flour for New Years Day
(tomorrow) when we expect to have a gala day 4 o.c. Ship
struck by a tremendous wave — our Skilly upset and
several scalded — 3 of our mess lost theirs — We're
shipping heavy seas every moment — very high sea.

1st January 1868 — Last night very rough — almost
impossible to sleep from rolling of ship — on deck early
this morning — some of the Convicts broke into the ships
stores last night and abstracted several articles (provinder)
one of them has been sentenced to be flogged tomorrow
— 12 o.c. S. lat 38° 13' E. long 99° 46' — 196 miles — 1
o.c. just after dining with N°1 Mess — we enjoyed a better
dinner than usual — having saved our provisions of
former day, after Dinner we sang 'We'll meet again
together' — 4 o.c. writing heading on the Xmass no of
'The Goose' (which we are to give to the Capt[n]) for past 2

hours in Priests cabin — weather getting beautiful — at work all day — a ship in sight — we're anxiously expecting to get to our journeys end by next Sunday — We are quite tired of our long voyage — Roll called tonight for the 1st time.

2nd All hands piped on Deck at 10 o.c. to be present at the punishment — I could not look at it — so John, Jack, Old Joe, and I talked & smoked till we got below again — the Man received 3 doz — a ship in sight — I have just finished 'The Goose' for Captn so I trust now to have a holiday — and write no more until I can write my dear K ashore — 12 o.c. S. lat 37° 11' E. long 101° 38' — 116 miles.

3rd January — when finishing the other side on Thursday Evg I thought I should not again resume my pen until I'd be writing to my dear K — but when the Captn got his Copy — the Mates would not rest satisfied until they also got Souvenirs of our 'Goose' so we are preparing copies of 1st & 4th No^s for them — I may as well amuse myself by jotting a few more words in my little book

4th (Friday) I turned out at 3.45 AM & went on deck at 4 o.c. with Jack & John — we had a fresh water wash and witnessed a most gorgeous Sunrise, perhaps the prettiest (but one) I have ever beheld — shortly after (thanks to the

generosity of a good friend) we breakfasted (at 5.45) off preserved Salmon — Biscuit & Coffee — we enjoyed it admirably had a chat & went below at 6. 9 o.c. we are now going to commence our fresh work — so here goes.

12 o.c. S. lat 36° 25' E. long 103° 39' — 107 miles — I helped Old Joe to day engraving on brass — A sail (A Spaniard from Liverpool to Manilla) has kept up with us for two days — beautiful weather — calm & warm, — Saturday — went on deck at 6.30 pm — Old Joe up hard a word cleaning our compartment all the morning — had supper — a most delightful sunset — below again at 7.30 pm where we — Jack, John, Dan, Sobersides, & I (& Tom) had a delicious entertainment, preserves — this has been quite a gala day — Old Joe & Dan are infatuated with 'Norah the pride of Kildare' & 'I've wandered in dreams' we sang them last night in beautiful style — of course (for the memories they awaken) I love them. I've been to confession to-day & hope for the happiness of receiving the blessed sacrament tomorrow

4th S.l. 35° 43' E.l. 105° 38' — 105 miles

5th (Sunday) I had the happiness of receiving the Holy Communion this morning — our Quire sang — beautiful warm weather — I have just seen shoals of Porpoises playing around the ship — the sight was beautiful — five or six in a row leap right out of the water together & chase each other thro the sea — a beautiful Sunset this Evg — Jack, John, Joe & I on deck till 7.30 12 o.c. S. lat 35° 8' E. long 107° — 76 miles — 465 miles off

6th (Twelfth Day) We have just had Mass celebrated —
Conv^S sang — the Spanish ship which we sighted some
days since is still with us — lime juice going to be served
— 12 o.c. S. lat 33° 40' E. long 107° 9' — 50 miles — A
shark measuring about 14 feet in length has just been (with
my help) pulled on board — he was seen swimming about
the ship — when a pork bait was thrown out — he took it
& was quickly pulled in — he was a terrible brute and
lashed right & left with his huge body and tail after
coming on board — he was pulled from the Forecastle &
to the Main deck, where his tail and <u>head</u> were cut off —
notwithstanding which he still dived about and lashed in
all directions with his huge trunk — even when the body
had been cut open he still rolled over and did not expire
until he was literally cut in pieces — a small fish was
taken from his entrails which is still alive — by jove what
a frightful mouth the beggar had — several pilot fish were
about him when he was captured — they always precede
him to discover pray [prey?] — Jack & several others have
got some of the skin to make cigar cases & tobacco
pouches [squiggle for 'etc.'] — Jack intends to cover a
Bible (which Father Delany presented him with) with a
part of the skin

7th January — I have been hard at work since 5.30 A.M.
finishing the copies of 'The Wild Goose' for the Mates &
have just completed them — thank goodness this at all
events will finish my penmanship for the voyage — 12 o.c.
S. lat 33° 26' E. long 108° 38' — 62 miles

We have been becalmed for the past few days — but a breeze has just sprung up which we believe will (if it continues) take us to Fremantle in <u>two</u> days more — Of course we are all conjecturing as to what sort of place our new abode will be — when we are to regain our liberty — and chalking out our future modes of life, my only hope is to earn money with as much expedition as possible and have my dearest K and dear boys with me where-ever I may pitch my tent as quickly as I possibly can — God grant that my ardent wish be accomplished.

8th The Anchors are getting ready — cables getting out from lockers — and all preparations being made for Fremantle — as we expect to arrive there early tomorrow, Joe, Dan, & I sang 'Norah' & 'I've Wandered' last night in splendid style — they're infatuated with the airs — I had to transcribe them to-day for them — as this is all I shall write at sea — I will (to make it more impressive) finish by praying God to bless my dearest Kathleen & my little boys — Denis

The following poems appear in this order following the diary proper, and were apparently written by the individual authors:

'To Denis B. Cashman, Esq.'*#	John Boyle O'Reilly
'Farewell'#	John Boyle O'Reilly
'The Green'#	John Boyle O'Reilly
'Hallow E'en'	John Flood
'To —'	John Flood
'Live it down'	John Flood
'Friendship'	Denis Cashman
'Louisa Hayden'	John Flood
'The Old School Clock'	John Boyle O'Reilly
'Cremona'	John Flood
'Cinderella'	John Flood
untitled ['French Prisoners']*#	John Boyle O'Reilly

(After O'Reilly's signature & date, there is
scrawled: 'Now, Denis, eh?')

These two poems are the only ones of those transcribed in the diary that did not appear in The Wild Goose. *They are included with the poems in the next section of this volume.*

#These four poems do not appear in the collected poems section of Roche's biography of O'Reilly (which was edited by his wife and does contain other unpublished pieces).

The following appears at the very end of the diary. There is no indication as to when it was written.

I believe I haven't mentioned anything of our treatment on board hitherto, so I may as well say a few words on the subject — We (the Fenians) had a separate Compartment in the Convict portion of the ship — we were very glad of this as the majority of the Convicts were the greatest ruffians, and most notorious robbers in England — Of course we did not associate or scarcely speak to the unfortunates, altho I believe a portion of them had been <u>very respectable</u> & well educated — a good many of them had a great respect for our men & endeavoured to show it by several acts of good nature & being most respectful in their deportment — Some of them were very notorious characters — Viz the Scuttlers of the Ship 'Severn' — the owner appeared a gentlemanly sort of fellow — the great Jewel robbers — the boy that stabbed his fellow apprentice — a cool murder — A fellow who killed his mother — in fact they were <u>all</u> an extremely proficient class at their <u>business</u>

Our food was pretty good i.e. biscuit & tea — with occasionally a change of chocolate for breakfast — pea soup, Salt Horse (i.e. Beef) & preserved potatoes (like beans, in an uncooked state) for dinner — instead of the soup we had plum duff 4 times a week — A glass of wine each at 2 o.c. — and Skilly (i.e. gruel) at 4 o.c. — this was our dietary scale — we did not have <u>near</u> sufficient to allay the appetite — merely sufficient to support life.

Any of the Convicts who misconducted themselves were put in irons — that is — an iron ring was welded round each ankle, to each of which was attached a chain — so that their steps had to be measured by the length of the chain — it was awful to hear the unfortunates — with the chains clanking every where they went — there were so many of them in them (the chains) that the clank was continuous on deck & below — they had to bring them to bed with them — as they did not get them off till the ship came to Anchor

On prison life I could fill a volume — but of course this is not the place — I will merely give you what 'Tom Bains' calls a 'wrinkle' on Convict audacity — In one of the yards at Millbank — I saw a Convict, aye with impunity, rob a gaolers pouche — the gaoler standing before him — facing him — and take all the tobacco in it — no more time — Goodbye My D^{rl}—

Following this entry appears a song written to be sung to the tune of 'Tramp! Tramp! Tramp!' It was written by Cashman and dedicated to his son, Willie. This song appears in the next section of this volume.

The Hougoumont Poems and Others

From Cashman's Diary

1st   To lonely dreams of grief I bend,
       Secluded thoughts of home so gay;
       Away from friends to exile send:
       In drooping years may — hope to lay.

2nd   Ah! brothers dear who'll dig the grave
       Or shed a tear as mother is in clay,
       I kiss that life upon the stormy wave;
       Bitter sighs mark my brow each day[.]

3rd   In sad decline my pulse do beat,
       Alas! freedom's strife no more to see;
       [Pangs?] so grave this heart-felt fate:
       With mourning sobs I weep for thee.

4th   Round my mind, shades of sorrow sleep;
       Low as dust 'neath the fellow's heel;
       For from the father land beyond the deep,
       Future hopes the fading past do feel.

5*th*   *With bosom smiles adieu to Innisfail,*
       This livid [hand?] I feel with vivid pain;
       Farewell! thy proud sou'll never wail
       Hard be the task while life remain.
6*th*   *Warm I love thee away oer the main,*
       None shall blush ne're didst cost a stain
       Bound in fetters I stretch my hand again,
       To die [without?] the [cursed?] chains.

To Denis Cashman
In token of our love and friendship during our acquaintance on board the convict ship, Hougoumont; so undying as never to be forgotten

Thomas McCarthy Fennell [signature]

To Denis B. Cashman, Esq.,
The following lines are dedicated, as testimony of our true and lasting friendship, formed on board the ship 'Hougoumont,' on our exile to Western Australia. Hereafter, should they bring back memories of those cloudy days, I trust that he will remember the few bright traits, and forget the many faults and foibles of his friend,

      John Boyle O'Reilly [signature]
      Jan 7th 1868. S.Lat 33° E.L. 108°

As you battle your way through the world
    And measure your own with its might,
In its face let your gauntlet be hurled,
    and boldly press on to the fight.

Let not failure your energies smother;
　　Unarmed, with adversity cope;
Let your motto be 'Honor,' my brother,
　　Your watchword and war-cry be 'Hope!'

On the right of your course be reliant,
　　And onward unswervingly steer;
Rise o'er worldly censures defiant,
　　Contemning the frown and the sneer.
And though bitter the draught of the trial,
　　On, brother, and quaff it with pride;
Though you drink to the dregs of the vial,
　　Still cherish the Truth for your guide.

Let not frowning misfortune appal you,
　　Nor shrink 'neath Calamity's rod;
Remember, whatever befal you
　　Is willed by an all-seeing God.
Act yourself, and ne'er trust to another;
　　When duty awaits never rest;
Look onward and upward, my brother,
　　And forget not, — what is, is the best.

JBOR [initials]

On hearing some news in Millbank that the *times were stirring at home*, I wrote the following lines to the stirring air of Tramp! Tramp! It was sung frequently at our Evening Concerts on board — Denis.

Air — 'Tramp! Tramp! Tramp! the boys are marching [']

When Evening's shadows fall. And the earth is robed in gray,
And Hesper's silver glimmer greets the moon;
Which in brightest lustre clad — sweetly pours a beaming ray;
Thro' my grated prison window's sombre gloom

— chorus

Then my day's hard toil being o'er, sitting in my dreary Cell,
Thoughts of Erin's wrongs, of wife, and children dear,
Moulds a tear — but not to fall; ne'er shall trickling moisture tell,
Of Celtic grief. No! Proud! defiant! *still* appear

My comrades brave I greet with a passive smile or sigh;
When to exercise our gaoler leads the way,
But I see the smouldering fire kindle in each glowing eye,
As the word is passed 'The Ball is up' Hurrah!

Then each step elastic threads, and each hand is tight compressed,
Each bosom swells, and fire the eyes emit
Burning is each noble breast. To have Ireland's wrongs redressed
And with vengeance feed the fire by Tyrants lit.

Then hurrah! for soon again in our Erin's vernal weather,
We'll be fanned by gentle Zephyrs from the Sea;
Which kiss upon the shamrocks fragrance, whispring softly thro'
     the heather
From our trans atlantic brothers. 'Celts be Free.'

Let no Swords bright sheen expire; no avenging arm tire;
Whilst a hated foe pollutes our sacred land,
Until Freedom reigns entire thrilling shout our war-cry higher,
Until Victory! Crowns our gallant Fenian Bands.

chorus after each verse

Hurrah! Hurrah! the green flag is unfurled,
Brave Fenian hearts are thronging to the fight;
Whilst their Slogan loud and shrill, echoes back from hill to hill,
As with flashing Steel they're tramping quick and light.

This is for Willy, — his father
Dns

From Cashman's Poetry Book

[The French Prisoners]

During the war with France in the beginning of this Century, the French prisoners of war were confined in Dartmoor Prison, Devonshire. During my sojourn there a tombstone was erected in their memory, their bones having been collected and placed in one grave. The following lines were written in my cell there, in August, 1867.

JBO'Reilly [signature]

A plaintive tale is briefly traced on yonder new-raised stones;
Tho' few the words, they seem to have a wailing weary tone
That well befits such tale as theirs — of suffering and of pain;
How brave men sank and died beneath the victor's galling chain.
Of blighted lives and blighted hopes, and hearts with anguish seared
They plainly speak, and gallant hearts grown sick with hope deferred.
Ah! sadder tale was never told — how that devoted band
Of captive soldiers drooped and died far from their sunny land.

How one by one they pined away, and prayed with latest breath
To heaven to bless their own loved France, then passed away in
    death.
But who may know what tender thoughts, of all brave men hold
    dear,
Of home, and friends, and loved ones lost, would force the swelling
    tear;
Or who may tell the dreams that crossed the captive's restless brains,
How some in sleep would wander to their far-off homes again;
How some would hear a father's voice — some feel a mother's kiss —
And one would see a maid he loved — Ah! then what rapturous
    bliss
Would thrall his heart and cause a smile to linger o'er his face
And drive the frown of waking times from its accustomed place.
Another to his Breton home would wander far away,
And see his dark-skinned gipsy lads around their cottage play;
And she — their mother — dark-eyed, too — upon his bosom pressed —
Ah! could he sleep and not awake that dreamer, too, were blessed.
And one — a very boy is he — goes wandering on and on
Oer well-known paths, until he sees his own, his loved Garonne.
Goes flashing thro' his native vale — and deep amongst the trees —
The home he left not long before with gladdened heart he sees.
Their sufferings past are all forgot — forgot the chafing chain —
His father, mother, brothers — all! he's with them once again!
Oh! would that we could leave them thus in pleasures unalloyed.
How dreadful must the waking be such blissful dreams destroyed!

But tender thoughts are not for all — yon sleepers troubled rest —
Is broken now with fiercer dreams of scenes <u>he</u> loved the best.
We seem to know his martial form — the very boot he wears
Proclaims him of the conquering corps — Napoleon's Grenadiers.
His place from very youth has been mid scenes of war and strife —
At home — abroad in camp and siege has passed his wandering
    life.

That swarthy face has felt the glare of many a burning sun,
Of far-off countries he could tell and glorious actions done.
But what scene of all the past rushing through his brain?
Whatever might be the direful strife he fights it o'er again.
His hands are clenched as o'er his mind the vivid picture flits
Say is it Lodi's bloodstained bridge — or glorious Austerlitz?
Yes, Yes, at Austerlitz is he — deep busied in the fray,
Amongst his brave old comrades, as he fought that dreadful day.
For hours they've stood unflinching as the deadly showers sped
But the fight is raging fiercer — swifter round them fall the dead.
Now they're moving swiftly forward. Hark! yon bugle's ringing
    peal —
They are running — they are charging with a terrific yell!
Charging on yon thick battalion pierced round with bristling steel —
But their Emperor gave the order — they can neither think nor feel.
They are dashing madly forward — Hah! the foe's loud volleys
    roar,
And their steady front is broken — but still madly on they pour.
Like some foaming mountain torrent dashing wild from rock to
    rock,
They are striking at the foemen, who are reeling 'neath the shock
Of those awful reeking bayonets — that are striking yet again
By heavens! in fight those Grenadiers were more than mortal men!
Now they see the foemen flying, and their fierce triumphant cheer
Of 'Vive Napoleon' follows, spreading panic thro' their rear.
Oh! they loved their daring leader — more than loved him — they
    adored!
They made very few distinctions — he was Emperor — he was Lord!
All the world might band against him, but they back defiance
    hurled
— He was <u>their own</u> — <u>their</u> Emperor — and for him they'd fight
    the world!
He knew the path they wished to tread — the path to Glory's scenes;
Oft he's made them <u>feel</u> that Glory in his thrilling bulletins.

Who like him could rouse to fury every simple soldier's heart?
Who could lead them on to conquest like their wondrous Bonaparte?
Sleep on, soldier! you deserved a death on some wide battle plain;
Sleep on, veteran! sleep, and dream your victories o'er again.
There are other forms around you lost to every waking grief;
They, like you, are following once again the footsteps of their chief.

Mark, yonder troubled slumberer — yon grim old Cuirassier —
Some fiercer emotion stirs his heart — no tender thoughts are these.
Draw closer! mark his war-worn face, how stern and wild it looks;
Neath Egypt's pyramids he fought the gorgeous Mamelukes.
They marked him, too — a fearful slash — from eye to lip it runs;
Oh! desperate cuts and deep they gave — those desert's fearless sons.
But say, where rides the trooper now — again across the sand;
Pursuing 'neath the burning sun some flying Arab band?
Or does he ride 'neath the milder skies o'er some Italian plain?
No, No, — on Austria's blood-stained soil the trooper rides again.
A glorious field all round him — once again the soldier hears
Napoleon's thrilling order — 'To the front, the Cuirassiers!'
Now boot to boot and bridles close their foaming steeds they urge,
And down upon the Austrian ranks those world conquerors charge.
Murat! the brave! the fearless! the King of Troopers! leads;
His voice is raised — his burning words their fierce excitement feeds
'The Emperor's eye is on us, men!' Hah! Sacre! on they go!
No human power could stand their shock — right thro' and thro'
        the foe
And thro' and thro' and back again, and wildly round they ride
And trample down the foemen whilst their hearts are filled with
        pride,
For they know that he is looking — He! their Emperor — nay, their
        God,
And their hands and hilts are dripping red with Austria's bravest
        blood
What cares he, then, what cares he, that brave old Cuirassier?

What cares now for England's claims or England's prisons drear?
The Emperor's eye is on him and Murat before him sweeps,
And the thrilling 'Charge!' is sounding tho' it be but while he sleeps!
Mark him now, he starts up wildly — now his step is on the floor,
And loud ringing thro' the prison goes his 'Vive l'Empereur!'
Now behold! the sleepers waken — yonder see those brave hussars
Have caught the thrilling echo, bringing back the glorious wars
Of their loved and daring leader, and again they see him stand,
Ruling o'er the countless armies he was born to command.
And their hearts are throbbing wildly, and their brains are all on fire,
And a mighty sound is swelling — swelling louder still and higher,
Till it bursts in one grand chorus of that glorious leader's name,
Swelling thro' that vaulted prison even as that leader's fame
Rang and swelled throughout the world! Oh! brave hearts! ye well
      deserved
To have served the noblest leader that a soldier ever served.
Ye have passed away before him, but e'en he will feel the weight
Of the crushing hand that killed you — like to yours will be his fate.
Now the Sceptred heads of Europe quail beneath his haughty
      glance
But he'll die a lonely exile many thousand leagues from France!
Sleep ye on, ye gallant soldiers! e'en in foreign soil ye'll rest
Till the mighty Trumpet calls you to the legions of the blest
There a brighter field will open will reward your sterling worth
And eternal bliss repay your true devotion here on earth.
Sleep ye on! ye need no pity! ye have died, but what is death
All your troubles, trials, perils, ended with your latest breath.

JBO'Reilly. [signature] 1st Jan. 1868

Now, Denis, eh?

[The Dead Who Died for Ireland]

The dead — who died for Ireland! Oh, these are living words
To nerve the hearts of patriots — to steel avenging swords.
They thrill the soul when spoken — and lowly bows the head
With reverence for the memories of all our martyred dead.

The dead — who died for Ireland! The7 noble ones — the best!
Who gave their lives for motherland — who poured upon her breast —
In freedom's cause — the blood she gave, — who with their dying
     breath
Sent prayers to God to heal her woes — then sealed their love in death.

The dead who died for Ireland! How hallowed are their graves!
With all their memories fresh and green, Oh! how could we be slaves!
How could we patient [clang?] the chain? How could we fawn
     and bow?
How could we crouch like mongrels 'neath their keepers frowning
     brows?

<u>Ye dare not</u>, men of Ireland! Ye dare not thus disgrace
The dead — who died for Ireland — the guardians of your race —
'Twere blackest sin to bear the yoke — 'twere crime to kiss the rod —
Their very blood would rise and cry for vengeance up to God.

The dead who died for Ireland! Ah! what a sea of woes
What depths of foul oppression do these sacred words enclose.
On the field and on the scaffold, and wherever men could die
They gave their priceless lives without a murmur or a sigh.

The dead — who died for Ireland! Oh! that they were still alive!
They would trample on the fetters, — they would break the accursed
     gyve.
They would fight for homes and altars — they would fight for
     name + race
But they're dead they died for Ireland! Who, Oh!, who will fill their
     place?

Be proud, ye men of Ireland! Be proud of those who died;
Never men oer all the earth had greater — nobler cause for pride.
Hope and strive, and league for freedom, and again the souls will
    rise
Of the dead who died for Ireland to cheer you to the prize.

The dead — who died for Ireland! Are beacons in the night
From the halo around their sacred graves we'll catch the holy light
That will beam on mother Erin when her sons no more are slaves
And the dead who died for Ireland shall sleep in freemen's graves.

[John Boyle O'Reilly]

After ['The French Prisoners'] and ['The Dead who Died for Ireland'], the remainder of the poems in Cashman's poetry book were not written by the Fenians. Some of the poems and authors — Poe's 'The Bells' and Macaulay's 'Horatius' — are well known, but the rest are not. They appear in the following order:

'The Bells' — Edgar Allen Poe
'Look at the Clock' — Revd Richd Barham, i.e., Thos Ingoldsby
'Lament for Shane O'Neill' — John Savage
'The Bridge of Sighs' — Thomas Hood
'Horatius' — Lord Macauley
'What is Tims?' — Marsden
'Lament for the Death of Eoghan Ruath O'Neill' — [Barham?]
'Barney MaGuires account of the Coronation' — Revd R. H. Burham

From John Flood's Notebook

To John Flood, Esq.

However mediocre the following lines may be, the feelings of admiration, respect, and friendship which prompted me to write them are deep and true; and by the worth of those feelings I know they will be received and judged. Hereafter, when our exile is ended, they may recall to Memory the beginning of our friendship And many pleasant (and busy) days we spent together over our little 'Wild Goose.'

John B. O'Reilly
December 12th, 1867
S.Lat 42° E.L. 10° 21'

Together, John, we're here tonight, —
Here on the wide, wide sea;
The waves around are whispering, John,
Good words to you and me.
Their words are words of strength and hope,
Though whispered soft and low:
We'll listen to their voices, John,
And learn us as we go.

'Look back upon your path,' they say;
'And learn from the past;
'Twill bear you on your rugged way,
Where'er your lot be cast.

Fenian Diary

Look back, look back, and flinch not
    Though the memory gives you pain;
See where and how you failed before,
    And never fail again.

Look back to those you left behind;
    Crush not the tender thrill,
That rises at a parent's name,
    Or one more cherished still.

Their love for you will never droop,
    Their prayers will ever rise,
Oh! cherish fondly in your hearts
    Such holy memories.

Look forward! Time is in your hands,
    Go mould the future well:
Be wise — be strong — be fearless men,
    And after times will tell

Your lives, your labours were not in vain;
    The end your works will prove.
Go live and love as brothers ought,
    With trust in God above.'
Their words are words of strength, John;
    We'll learn from the past,
And every holy thought of home
    We'll cherish to the last.

We'll live as brothers ever, John,
    Though severed we may be;
Forgetting not those soft low tones —
    Those whisperings of the sea.

The Wild Geese

Oh 'tis ages since the Wild Geese
First fled southward oer the main
To the battle fields of sunny France
And the olive hills of Spain —
Fled away before the tempest
From its lurid lightning gleam,
That fell upon their Sireland
Oh Sweet 'Erin of the Streams'

Oh long ages since have vanished
Still the tempest plague is there —
Still away their flight is winging
Still their cry is on the air
That cry caught from their fathers
In the days before their flight.
At Benburt and Bealan a [Burdhe?]
They screamed it in the fight.

And well they treasured up the sound
And shrieked it forth with joy
Upon the bloody battle fields
Raniellies and Fontenoy.
When France[']s chivalry was broke
How bright their pinions gleamed
As swooping on their hated foe
Their honor they redeemed.

It swelled again to victory
At Steinkirk and Oudinard

Once more on *Lauden's* plain it broke
But then it's joy was marred;
Their bravest noblest leader chief
Lay bleeding on the sod
Who grieved 'twas not for home he died
Then winged his soul to God.

Oh the Wild Geese the Wild Geese
Strong of wing and keen of sight
Ever sagest in the Council,
Ever strongest in the fight,
Ever South or West in battle
When their eagles [turned?] pale
Still flowed the tide of victory
Where their cry was on the gale.

Oh 'tis glorious to remember
Their brightest deeds from first to last
In Europe or *America*
Where they fled before the blast
Nor less glorious is the memory
Of those who for *Fatherland*
Struck down by felon laws
Died by a felon hand

Upon the scaffold curst they died
But in Ireland's soil they rest
Like children in their mothers arms
Thrice glorious and thrice blest —
And some they pined away in chains
As are others pining now
But chains could not their spirit break
Chains their proud souls couldn't bow

Oh the Wild Geese Oh the Wild Geese
Still their cry is on the gale
Gathering like a vengeful storm
While their foemen turning pale
As its dreadful cry of vengeance
Sounds like terror on the blast
Well they feel the day of reckoning
For their deeds has come at last

And that cry of ringing vengeance
It has reached across the foam —
Has fallen on the listening ears
Of those who pray at home —
On the ear of lovely maiden
On the heart of fervid youth
And her tears are dried with gladness
While his eyes are fired with [Truth?]

Oh the Wild Geese Oh the Wild Geese
They are coming back again
They are gathering East and South and West
Far across the stormy main
And once more shall Freedom's pinions
Shed their bright and glorious beams
When their cry is upward ringing
Oer Sweet 'Erin of the Streams' —

[John Flood]
[4 Dec 1867, probably]

My Star

The song and the laugh and the merry jest
 Fall sad on my heart tonight,
And I turn away on a plank to rest
 Alone in the pale moon light —
That falls with a ghastly and steady glare
 Aslant through the latticed bars —
With closed ears, for each boisterous air
 Tonight my spirit jars —
My thoughts are cold and as pale as the light
 That streams on the deck below;
They come like ghosts of memory's night —
 Fell phantoms of grief and woe.
My heart, like a ship on a troubled main,
 Is tossed on their rushing tide
That flows o'er the shallows and rocks of pain
 Their depths have failed to hide —
Slow the pale moon beams have stolen away,
 I watched them each fade and die,
And grown dark as a cell without a ray
 Is my heart in its agony;
But the cool wind plays on my burning brow,
 And whispers of better things.
And as one from a dream awakening now,
 I list as it murmuring sings:
'Look up, oh! look up, thou desponding heart'!
 And I turn my eyes above,
And there, oh, bright beautiful star! thou art
 With trembling rays of love:
Sweet star, oh how blessed thy bright rays fall
 Like balm on my troubled soul.

Thy dear beams in my darkest hours recall
　　Delight, that the onward roll
Of Time hath concealed in the far dim past —
　　Of my boyhood's early days
Sweet dream, of life, of spring [time?] that fled too fast
　　With its hawthorne scented days
And of [manhood's?] [with?] fervid summer time,
　　When loved and beloved again,
I sailed into its tropical clime
　　To voyage across life's main —
Sweet scenes of my childhood's shadowy eves,
　　When first to my heart you spoke,
And like the rustle of perfumed leaves,
　　A voice in my heart awoke.
So Dreamy and sweet, 'twas a voice of bliss —
　　Like music I hear it now,
As I feel the rays, like an angel's kiss,
　　Fall brightly upon my brow
Enchanting thoughts of life's springtime's years,
　　When a glory I saw thee rise
Ere my heart had yet felt life's scalding tears —
　　Tears that flow not from the eyes —
Amid scenes that lie, oh! so far away
　　From my prison home to-night —
By the lovely shores of sweet Dublin Bay
　　And Ben Eder's crownèd height,
Behind whose hills oft I have seen thee rise
　　Out shining calm, bright, and strong,
A beacon of light to more blissful skies.
　　[When?] a thrilling silver gong,
The voice of my boyhood, ringing out,
　　My soul fills with wild delight,
And stronger its wing at each joyous shout
　　In its yearning upward flight —

Of still brighter scenes of my manhood's days —
      That summer for ever fled —
The memory now of whose joy outweighs
      The sorrow to which it led.
And of days still later to which belong
      Thoughts checkered with bliss and pain,
When thy voice like a trumpet said, 'Be strong —
      Strong in heart and soul and brain.'
And above to-night like a talisman,
      Far from all I've loved and known,
Thou shinest still brighter and fairer than
      In those golden days long flown.
Shine down into the shadowy deeps
      Of my faint and weary heart,
Awakening the mystic voice that sleeps
      With a joyous thrilling start;
And thro' heart and brain loud it peals and swells
      A rapturous organ strain:
Whilst thy beams light up my heart[']s darkest cells
      With hope and strength and joy again.
Oh star of my strength, still shine upon
      The wavering path of my life,
Like an Angel[']s eye you have ever shone
      My courage in worldly strife.
Oh still shine down on life's troubled sea[,]
      A beacon with twofold ray;
Lighting up the Past to fond memory,
      And the Future[']s hidden way.

                    [John Flood]   10-12-67

Miscellaneous

Robert Emmet
(A narrative ballad of 1803. By D.B. Cashman)

'Sit down awhile
And let us once again assail your ears.'
— Shakespeare

Dear Erin! sob your tale of woe,
So sad, so grand, so feeling,
Into the hearts of friend and foe,
For it is just that they should know
Your sorrows, so appealing
To manly breasts for sympathy.
For who has suffered such as thee?
Let Robert Emmet be your theme,
Whose young life on the gibbet-beam
Was sacrificed to set you free.

The slaughter had ended of famed ninety-eight.
The patriot forces had met their sad fate,
And those who escaped — though beaten — were then
Awaiting some hero to lead them again.

The shadow of death threw its pall o'er the land,
For the tyrant still clutched in his merciless hand
The throat of the nation that dared to protest
'Gainst his murders, his rapine, his evil behest.

With gibbet and lash the redcoats persecuted
The people all over the land they polluted.

William Pitt, Castlereagh, vowed they ne'er would relinquish
Their horrors, till National Life they'd extinguish.

To the heart of old Erin a shudder was sent,
She was beaten — not cowed — as her opponent meant.
'Twas five years of dull sleep, ere again she awoke
To renew a great effort to throw off the yoke.

Out from Trinity's College Halls
Like a soldier brave when honor calls,
As an eaglet bold and daring;
Whose pinions swift, waft to the sky
To view the sun with fearless eye,
Young Emmet came with ardor high
No foeman's prowess fearing,
Nor for his vengeance caring.

He saw the land he loved so well
Was blighted, as with blasts from hell,
The countless wounds; the bitter tear;
Her heroes dead; her children's dread;
Her valor crushed; her genius fled;
To valiant France for aid he sped,
To meet with Irish exiles there,
Who then were scattered everywhere.

With hope high pulsing for his land
He pleaded earnestly for aid.
Napoleon sits with Talleyrand
To hear the plans young Emmet laid.

The consul's brow is knit with thought;
He hears the pleader's fervid tale,
And gives the promise that was sought,
'An expedition soon would sail.'

Back from the consul with heart on fire,
Young Emmet speeds, to rouse son and sire.
To prepare for a struggle with Erin's foes,
And grapple the tyrants that caused her woes.

With energy swift, sublime, and grand,
He kindled a flame throughout the land,
Till sixteen counties had promised to rise
And avenge the blood that to heaven cries.

> The mountain torrent that sweeping on
> From the melting snows of the spring
> Through its maddening course is singing its song,
> Till through peaceful meadows it glides along;
> It dances and sparkles, not ceasing to sing,
> Giving joy to valleys, and birds on the wing.

So Emmet, intensed, with his soul aflame,
Aroused the war-spirit wherever he came,
Impetuous, fiery, working to band
The men that remained in his stricken land;
Yet, his gentle speech, and his tender ways
Won all true hearts, and set souls ablaze.

The night was fixed when the rockets would fly
At nine o'clock, twenty-third of July.
That would give the signal to patriot bands
Who silently watched for their leader's commands.

But no signal flamed across the gloom,
No carbine's call; no cannon's boom.
For a traitor had taken the British gold
And like Judas Iscariot, his leader sold.

Fenian Diary

His plans were well laid, his points of attack,
His lines of defence; his points of check,
But the traitor spies had been on his track,
And deceived the men ready to come at his beck.

Kilwarden and Wolfe were slain in the street
Through which Emmet marched, his foes to meet.
And heaps of dead lay stretched in the Coombe
Where Colonel Brown and his men met their doom.

But the traitor's art was plied so well,
That those who fought, and those who fell
Without their leader rushed blindly on
And lost the victory they could have won.

Deceived! Betrayed! Oh, who shall say
The agony he felt that day?
His soul was stricken as by a blight,
And fled his hopes of freedom's fight.

'Oh, had I another week!' he cried,
One thousand pounds and one thousand men,
All England's power I would have defied,
And won! I would have feared nothing then.'

For a month he eluded both soldier and spy,
Who were close on his track full often.
Ah! what keeps him ling'ring where danger is nigh?
'Tis his lady-love — he will see her or die;
Ere he quits his land he'll all danger defy
For one word of that love that could soften
The anguish keen that he felt in his heart
For having from country and love soon to part.

He hovered near her dwelling place
With fervid expectation
To see her tread the well-known walks
Where love once fed their ardent talks;
But death behind him grimly stalks
    With grinning exultation.
She came not there to give solace
To her love — the noblest of his race.

The traitor spy had tracked him down
Like a sleuth-hound for the British crown,
        One thousand pounds his synecdoche,
        The rest for Sirr, the Irish Fouche.
Foul Major Sirr, without time's loss,
Arrested Emmet in Harold's Cross.

There is wailing throughout the Island,
Bitter grief in dale and highland,
For the noblest son of Erin is delivered to his fate.
Ah, they know full well the sorrow
That will be theirs on the morrow,
For the British never pardon those surrendered to their hate.

Oh! the bullet, rope, and bayonet,
And the axe they plied, and meant it
To depopulate a nation bold, that erst was great and free.
For long years the bloody slaughter
Was kept up, while o'er the water
They deported men by thousands to far islands in the sea.

His trial soon came. Lord Norbury,
The 'bloody' judge, much longed to see
The noble victim of his malice
Now doomed to drink the bitter chalice.

The farce of trial, with jury packed
With Orangemen, who would have racked
The soul from every honest man
Who'd dare for freedom's cause to plan.

From 10 A.M. till 10 at night
The farce went on. Oh! what a sight!
A pack of wolves with eager jaws,
Pretending to mete out just laws.
No layman's garb was seen in court —
All military, wigs and gowns,
A veritable British fort,
Where mercy's blind and justice frowns.

McNally, the prisoner's counsel, e'en
Was a sworn enemy of the green,
A man receiving secret pay
To trap fresh victims night and day.
Alas! brave Emmet! no mercy you'll see
Till you face your Judge in Eternity.

The evidence in, in the usual way
They asked. 'Now, therefore, what have you to say
Why judgment of death and execution
Should not be awarded according to law
Against you?' O God! what base pollution
To name such forms of vile see-saw,
For, without leaving the box, the jury found
The prisoner Guilty! on every ground.

It was then that Emmet's soul broke out in flame
Of speech that has won him immortal fame:

'When my spirit shall have joined
Those bands of martyred heroes
Who have shed their blood
On the scaffold and in the field
In defence of their country,
This is my hope:
That my memory and name may serve
To animate those who survive me.'

Here Norbury began to scold
And lecture Emmet for being so bold.
Four times ere this he preached repentance
Eager to pass the dreadful sentence,
When he mentioned poor Emmet's dear father's name
That heart on fire again burst into flame:

If the spirits of the illustrious dead
Participate in the concerns of those who were dear to them
In this transitory scene,
Dear shade of my venerated father,
Look down on your suffering son
And see has he for one moment
Deviated from the moral and patriotic principles
Which you so early instilled into his youthful mind,
And for which he has now to offer up his life
My lord you are impatient for the sacrifice;
The blood which you seek is not congealed
By the artificial terrors which surround your victim.
It circulates warmly and unruffled through its channels,
Be yet patient!
I have but a few more words to say.

I am going to my cold silent grave;
My lamp of life is nearly extinguished;
I have parted with everything

That was dear to me in this life,
And for my country's cause;
With the idol of my soul, the object of my affections,
My race is run; the grave opens to receive me,
And I sink into its bosom!

I have but one request to ask
At my departure from this world.
It is the charity of silence.
Let no man write my epitaph;
For as no man who knows my motives
Dare now vindicate them,
Let not prejudice or ignorance asperse them.

Let them rest in obscurity and peace!
Let my memory be left in oblivion
And my tomb remain unsubscribed
Until other times and other men
Can do justice to my character.

When my country takes her place
Among the nations of the earth,
Then, and not till then,
Let my epitaph be written. I have done.'

It was ten o'clock that fatal night,
The nineteenth of September.
The Green street court, with its candlelight,
Was dim and spectral to the sight —
    A weird scene to remember.
Full often from that awful place
The noblest men of the Irish race
Left bloody tracks, from which we trace
    Their dolorous way to the scaffold.

Young Emmet stood beside his grave,
Defiant, fearless, noble, brave!
His counsel sued with all his skill
For two days' respite ere they kill
Their victim; but it was refused.
Norbury smiled — he was not used
Such acts of mercy to give the accused.
From such a source, of hope no ray
Could come. He dies! at one next day.

To Newgate prison they hurried him off
From that shamble and butcher and his staff.
When the iron fetters were on each leg,
In a condemned cell he was placed by Gregg.
But the Castle watch-dog never sleeps;
For the victim doomed a vigil he keeps.

In the lonely hours of that dreadful night,
When the clouds shut out the pale moon's light,
He was dragged from the prison without demur,
And was sent to Trevor, the inquisitor.
From Caiphas to Pilate, who did not fail
To safely secure him in Kilmainham jail.

That morning's dawn had scarcely broke, and ere the prison bell
Had clanged its dreary tones to rouse the dreamer in each cell,
Among them scores of patriots whose fate uncertain lay
At the mercy of the tyrant and his whim from day to day,
A stealthy form is gliding softly through the prison gloom.
At Emmet's dungeon door now it stops. The silence of the tomb
Pervades the place, when suddenly, the door is open swung,
And Trevor jumps inside, and round his baleful look he flung.

He found a noble prisoner, so calm and free from fear.
With a fork fixed in the table, from which hung a tress of hair.
He was braiding it with loving hands to wear beside his heart;
Sweet relic from his lady-love, from whom that day he'd part.
But oh! the cruelty! the shame! they sent an evil breath —
McNally, the false hireling — to announce his mother's death.
Her gentle spirit, rent with grief, the previous day had gone,
And waited near in the atmosphere to join her best loved son.

And on the table by which he sat, next to the tress of golden hair,
A severed head, the trunk, the axe, and the rope was lying near.
'Twas a faithful likeness of himself, a sketch of all the horrors
So soon to come; but it showed he had robbed death of all its terrors.
They pinioned his hands and led him forth. No loving friend was
*   there,*
To bid him a last and long farewell, or drop a silent tear.
One man — a humble turnkey, whose tears were falling fast —
Touched Emmet's heart. Much moved, he stopped and kissed him
*   as he passed.*

The man who was the one in charge of Emmet's last retreat,
And loved the noble prisoner, fell senseless at his feet.

From the prison the cortege moves slowly away;
The sherrifs, the hangman, the warlike array
Of dragoons, horse and foot, in their gaudy display,
All guarding one man who had offered his life
In freedom's dear cause and its uncertain strife,
And for whom death now waited and would not be baffled,
With his scythe grimly resting upon the scaffold.

In a carriage waiting in the street was a lady pale and tearless,
With agonized face, from the window she bent.
'Tis Sarah Curran, whose soul was rent;
*   His idol, his lady-love peerless.*

Emmet saw the loved vision, and, with a start
Saw that death's cold grip was clutching her heart.
    Oh! the pity that thus they should meet,
When, in a few minutes, forever they'd part,
And those few dreaded minutes so soon to fleet.

They waved to each other a sad farewell,
And a long, lingering look, while her bosom's swell
Showed the bursting agony which she felt —
An agony which no tears would melt,
For death's cold hand congealed the font,
And no softening balm from its source would mount.

Arrived at the gibbet in Thomas street,
The troops surrounded its awful feet.
Brave Emmet ascends with fearless [mien ?].
Ah! never before greater hero was seen,
    A few simple words he uttered then:
    'I die in peace with good will to all men.'
Then a cry of pain from the hearts was wrung,
As to eternity brave Emmet was flung.

    His last request was flouted down
    By hirelings of the British crown,
In the green uniform of his country to die,
And with it in his coffin forever to lie.
    They sneered and refused; his blood should be
    His gory shroud for Eternity.
One convulsed tremor, and two spirits arise
To their God and His home in the distant skies.

Scarce was the soul from the body riven,
And while floating off to its place in heaven,
When the body was flung from the lofty gibbet

To pay the British its bloody tribute.
The headman's axe struck off the head,
And poured out the blood of the martyred dead.

Then gripping the dripping head by the hair,
    The headsman raised it in the air,
Proclaiming aloud from that bloody theatre:
        'This is the head of a traitor!
            Robert Emmet.'

A traitor! Yes, to their cursed laws,
But a patriot-martyr in Ireland's cause,
Whose noble blood to Heaven still cries,
And bids her brave sons to awake, to uprise!
And in one gallant effort to throw off their thrall
And win freedom, or else — in her strife to fall.

A traitor? Yes! So were all heroes that fell,
Or that fought for freedom throughout the world.
Washington, Emmet, Kosciosco, Tell!
Were traitors, indeed when their flags were unfurled.
But ah! Great God! The dogs are lapping
The sacred blood that the ground is sapping.

        Ye millions of men of the Irish race,
        Whenever scattered, all over the earth
        Will ye not prepare for the time to trace
        As Freemen! in the land of your birth.
            On noble tomb and cenotaph,
            Immortal Emmet's Epitaph!

The Patriot's Grave

(Read at the Emmet Centennial in Boston, March 4, 1878)

I

*Tear down the crape from the column! Let the shaft stand white
    and fair!*
Be silent the wailing music — there is no death in the air!
We come not in plaint or in sorrow — no tears may dim our sight:
We dare not weep o'er the epitaph we have not dared to write.

Come hither with glowing faces, the sire, the youth, and the child;
This grave is a shrine for reverent hearts and hands that are undefiled;
Its ashes are inspiration; it giveth us strength to bear,
And sweepeth away dissention, and nerveth the will to dare.

*In the midst of the tombs, a Gravestone — and written thereon no
    word!*
*And behold, at the head of the grave, a gibbet, a torch, and a
    sword!*
And the people kneel by the gibbet, and pray by the nameless stone
*For the torch to be lit, and the name to be writ, and the sword's red
    work to be done!*

II

With pride and not with grief
We lay this century leaf
Upon the tomb, with hearts that do not falter:
A few brief, toiling years
Since fell the nation's tears,
And lo, the patriot's gibbet is an altar!

The people that are blest
Have him they love the best
To mount the martyr's scaffold when they need him;
And vain the cords that bind
While the nation's steadfast mind,
Like the needle to the pole, is true to freedom.

III

Three powers there are that dominate the world —
Fraud, Force, and Right — and two oppress the one:
The bolts of Fraud and Force like twins are hurled —
Against them ever standeth Right alone.

Cyclopian strokes the brutal allies give:
Their fetters massive and their dungeon walls;
Beneath their yoke, weak nations cease to live,
And valiant Right itself defenceless falls!

Defaced is law, and justice slain at birth;
Good men are broken — malefactors thrive;
But, when the tyrants tower o'er the earth,
Beneath their wheels strong right is still alive!

Alive, like seed that God's own hand has sown —
Like seed that lieth in the lowly furrow,
But springs to life when wintry winds are blown:
To-day the earth is gray — 'tis green to-morrow.

The roots strike deep despite the ruler's power,
The plant grows strong with summer sun and rain,
Till Autumn bursts in deep red-hearted flower,
And freedom marches to the front again!

While slept the right, and reigned the dual wrong,
    Unchanged, unchecked, for half a thousand years,
In tears of blood we cried, 'O Lord, how long?'
    And even God seemed deaf to Erin's tears.

But when she lay all weak and bruised and broken,
    Her white limbs seared with cruel chain and thorn —
As bursts the cloud, the lightning word was spoken,
    God's seed took root — His crop of men was born!

With one deep breath began the land's progression:
    On every field the seeds of freedom fell:
Burke, Grattan, Flood, and Curran in the session —
    Fitzgerald, Sheares, and Emmet in the cell!

Such teachers soon aroused the dominant nation —
    Such sacrifice insured an endless fight:
The voice of Grattan smote wrong's domination —
    The death of Emmet sealed the cause of right!

IV

Richest of gifts to a nation! Death with the living crown!
Type of ideal manhood to the people's heart brought down!

Fount of the hopes we cherish — Test of the things we do;
Gorgon's face for the traitor — Talisman for the True!

Sweet is the love of a woman, and sweet is the kiss of a child;
Sweet is the tender strength, and the bravery of the mild;

But sweeter than all, embracing all, is the young life's peerless price —
The young heart laid on an altar, as a nation's sacrifice.

How can the debt be cancelled? Prayers and tears we may give —
But how recall the anguish of hearts that have ceased to live?

Flushed with the pride of genius — filled with the strength of life —
Thrilled with delicious passion for her who would be his wife —

This was the heart he offered — the upright life he gave —
This is the silent sermon of the patriot's nameless grave.

Shrine of a nation's honor — stone left blank for a name —
Light on the dark horizon to guide us clear from shame —

Chord struck deep with a keynote, telling us what can save —
'A nation among nations,' or forever a nameless grave.

Such is the will of the martyr — the burden we still must bear;
But even from death he reaches the legacy to share:

He teaches the secret of manhood — the watchword of those who
aspire —
That men must follow freedom though it lead through blood and fire;

That sacrifice is the bitter draught which freemen still must quaff —
That every patriotic life is the patriot's epitaph.

[John Boyle O'Reilly]

The following poem was written by John Boyle O'Reilly on 19 November 1869, as the ship *Bombay* sailed into Delaware Bay. O'Reilly gave the poem to the *Bombay*'s captain, F.C. Jordan of Brunswick, Maine. The family kept the poem until a grandson, W.T.A. Fitzgerald, sent it to *The Boston Post*, which published it on 15 December 1944.

The Bombay

Fair to look on, light and graceful,
  but as strong as flexile steel —
True and trusty is the Bombay,
  from her royals to her keel.
Like a slave who loves his master,
  ever eager to fulfill
Every task imposed, she answers
  to her brave commander's will.

As a maiden trusts her lover,
  so she trusts, as if she knew,
That his wisdom was her safeguard,
  and his love her guardian, too.
Ah, coquette! She knows her worth
  is prized; she knows, or seems to know,
That her master will not ask her
  more than she can well bestow.

And she's worth his love; she proves it,
  where the hoarse wind sweeps the sea,
Seeming bent to dash her fiercely
  'gainst the dark rocks on her lee —
Then to see her! How she bends
  beneath the tempest's angry mood.
Still she wins an inch and holds it,
  till she makes her offing good.

Or far off upon mid-ocean —
  'tis the wildest hour of all —
When she battles with the great waves —
  when she fights the howling squall
When her broad wings are all folded —

when for days there comes no lull —
Then she's faithful — then she proves it,
as she rides it like a gull!

And tomorrow when 'tis over,
and her course again she steers,
Just as graceful, as if she were
built for nought but gentle airs.
Ah! No brave ship e're topped a sea;
she never tries to top.
But great or small, just let them come —
The Bombay will never stop.

To fall and rise — straight on she goes,
and meets them with her bow.
She strikes them like a pugilist —
she cuts them like a plough —
Hah, sail away, you good ship!
May you live a brave old life!
Stem the currents, fight the tempests
and be victor in the strife.

May no death blow ever reach you,
may that hearse wind never come
With a swoop of awful triumph
as it drives you to your doom.
May the great waves never whelm you,
may the howling squall pass o'er.
And leave you riding proudly,
good and trusty as before.

May you bear your master always
a[s] through perils past away
And whatever sea you sail upon —
God bless you, old Bombay.

'To Capt, F.C. Jordan of the Bombay with a sincere wish for his welfare and happiness, this little piece, worthless as it is, was written with every feeling that one man can possess who admires and esteems another.

'(signed) J. Boyle O'Reilly
Delaware Bay — Nov. 19th., 1869'

Why Fear to Die?

'To His likeness' ye are made! behold
In man His wondrous power he did unfold!
The noblest of his works! The godlike soul
Far greater than the glorious spheres that roll
In dazzling light through space supernal
Decay they must, but the soul's eternal.

II

From out the earth each hour and minute,
Dart countless souls to the great infinite;
From town and village, sea and shore;
From where war's cruel cannons roar,
Incessant streaming from the world
Through endless space are the millions hurled.

III

We see our dear ones vanish one by one;
A year — a day — and we, too, will be gone;
Whither? we ask in doubt and dread. To where
Is calm repose, or where man's fear
Says all is horror; where the chastening rod
Is swung by demons or withheld by God?

IV

Alas, we know not, but we feel the good
Who live believing that the Saviour's blood
For them was lavished; who sin repent,
And shall meet forgiveness through this sacrament,
Shall find a blissful rest. To all 'tis given
Believing thus to merit Heaven.

V

Too true, the hand of death the bravest fear;
E'en nature shudders when the reaper's near.
Yet 'tis but a gasp, and the soul takes flight,
From doubt and darkness to eternal light.
To His bright presence, whence the souls have fled,
Of countless millions by the angels led.

VI

Why fear to die? — a month — a day;
We're e'en forgotten ere we reach the clay.
The air that throbs with the shouts of the brave
Who march from their tents to the open grave,
Scarce echoes the sound of the fierce attack
When oblivion shrouds their last bivouac.

VII

We, too, are marching away from camp,
Our path illumined by a flickering lamp
(While the sexton digs with tireless breath)
Till the flame blows out, and we're grasped by death.
Still we'll boldly tread, though the grave be nigh,
God's peace awaits us. Why fear to die?

Denis B. Cashman

Nature's Book

From sea to sea, from shore to shore,
From earth to sky where saints adore,
From mountain peaks where eagles soar,
    A book is spread:
A book that opens to man's thought
The wond'rous secrets God has wrought
Since Satan with great Michael fought
    His battle dread.

The cosmos to our finite gaze
In mystery holds our deep amaze,
While to the great Creator praise
    We send on high.
Stupendous wonders everywhere,
On earth, in sky, on sea, in air;
And He, their maker, ever near
    With watchful eye.

Sustaining all the life that teems
From out the earth, or glides through streams,
Effulgently His sun's bright beams
    On all are shed.
The forest tree, the slender flower,
The things that start to life each hour,
Man, insect, beast, reveal His power
    Majestic, dread.

This open book to man is given
To read and win his way to heaven,
While through life's stormy sea he's driven,
  Unsteer'd the while:
That reading he may win the goal,
By steering safe through waves that roll,
Until in triumph speeds his soul
  To God's sweet smile.

From sun to sun, while night holds sway,
And cosmic gems their light display,
The trembling orbs in bright array
  Show wonders rare.
Eternal Space reveals to eyes
Uplifted to the far-off skies,
In panoply that never lies,
  The secrets there:

Processions greater than our minds
  Can grasp, of spheres of nobler kinds
Than earth, our home, which in them finds
  Its borrowed light,
The heavens speak through portals wide
Their secrets deep in man confide;
To join the hosts that there abide
  Our souls invite.

Yet this great book, so nobly planned,
And written plainly by God's hand,
Through fairest sky, on sea, on land,
  We rarely scan.
Our little schemes of selfish life
Absorb our thought, urge on our strife
To win our ends; nought else is rife
  In heart of man.

And yet, when won, contentment never
Satisfies each gained endeavor;
The anxious quest for ever — ever,
    Has voids to fill.
Although life's spans may be near run,
'Tis eager as when first begun,
Ne'er satisfied with triumphs won,
    No, not until

That spirit, freed from life's embrace,
Wings its swift way to where God's grace
In other spheres shall find a place
    For it to dwell.
Content shall then, and only then,
Our guerdon be, but only when —
Our lives deserving — the Angel's pen
    Saves us from hell.

Then read the book so nobly planned
And written by God's holy hand,
And do the things that His command
    Tells us to do,
That so the Angel's pen may measure
By God's sweet grace a heav'nly treasure,
That shall for ever prove a pleasure
    To me and you.

Denis B. Cashman

A Vision

An angel form, in a gleam of light,
Came down from the stars, on a clear, calm night,
To a lonely spot, where the tall grass waves
In tangled masses above the graves.

A hand as bright as the living flame
Laid a rose on a mound without a name;
A rose that grew in a garden high,
In a star that smiled from the distant sky.

Can I buy a wreath for that grave I love?
Can I place some flowers or an emblem dove
Where my children are laid, 'neath the damp, cold clay?
Like others, on Decoration Day.

To them the privilege is not given,
He said; but the rose that flowered in heaven
Is there, where the angel's hand was placed,
On the lonely grave where no name is traced.
'Tis there. 'Tis there.

Denis B. Cashman

'Tribute of a Co-Mate in Exile

Poem Written by Denis B. Cashman
in Memory of John Boyle O'Reilly

The following tribute in verse was prepared by one who was present, though taking no active part, yesterday, in the dedication of the monument to John Boyle O'Reilly, but who had been associated with him intimately under various relations in Australia, on the Convict ship, and in America, Mr. Denis B. Cashman, who, while on the ocean, edited with O'Reilly the unique journalistic offspring of the sea, 'The Wild Goose':

Mens Divinor — O'Reilly

Each century great men are born
Whose thoughts and acts their time adorn:
In every age, across the sky
Of vision, like bright meteors fly
Some names, that blaze in rapid flight
Illuming hist'ry's page with light.

Great deeds, like sparks of fire from some
Who armies led and battles won:
Bright thoughts from more, with genius' rays
Flamed out, and lit those far-off days,
Each brilliant deed and thought enhanced
Men's progress, through his slow advance.

But ah! the poet in tender song,
Sunshine and music sent along,
Through every spot of earth it roamed,

And like the billows, oft' it foamed
Around, and beat the rocks whereon
Is maimed, or wrecked, poor hapless man.

The poet shall live in song he made
When lustre from the great shall fade.
Prismatic thought whose genial rays
Bloomed into flowers with circling bays
Shall live and thrill in music sweet,
Through hearts that live, till souls shall fleet.

The gentle heart that beat for those
　　　Who sorrow's cross had borne,
Though stilled in death's last sad repose
On suffering still its pulse bestows
Through deathless thought that once uprose,
　　　And pleads for all who mourn.

Then let the bronze and stone unite
Their living story to indict,
And laud the poet's art divine,
And shamrocks with the bays entwine;
While shrined his chords in human heart
His fame and name shall ne'er depart.

When purged through the storm
On board the convict ship
While lightnings flashed and thunders crashed
And prayer was on each lip,
We grasped each other's hand
And promised friendship true
When from the southern-cross and albatross
We'd take our last adieu.

Fenian Diary

The Hougoumont to anchor came
Off Fremantle — that dreaded name
Whose coral reefs are shunned by all
Who sail the seas. And then the pall
Of darkened convict life o'ercast
O'Reilly and myself at last.

But guided by God's holy hand
We met again in this free land
Where he won honors, hearts and merit
Sweet rest and peace be with his spirit.

Denis B. Cashman

Notes

1. Research for this book was conducted at various libraries in Boston, MA, and various libraries and archives in Ireland and Northern Ireland, on grants from the Irish American Cultural Institute and East Carolina University. Denis B. Cashman's original diary is in the Manuscript Collection at East Carolina University; the copies in other libraries are, in some places, incomplete and/or incorrect. References to the Cashman diary in this text are by date of entry.

2. The firm of Dobbyn & Tandy, although no longer owned by a member of either original family, is still in business in Waterford.

3. In fact, the American Fenians tried twice, in 1866 and in 1870, to invade Canada, liberate it from England, and use it as a base from which to free Ireland. Neither attempt was strongly supported by Irish-Americans.

4. Cashman and O'Reilly later worked together at *The Pilot* in Boston; John Flood's conditional pardon required him to stay in Australia. There, among other pursuits, he edited *The Irish Citizen* in Sydney and, after moving to Cooktown, Queensland, edited *The Cooktown Courier*; he later worked on the *Brisbane Courier* and still later became controlling proprietor of *The Gympie Miner* ('Papers Pertaining to John Flood'; Amos 280). Flood, like O'Reilly and Cashman, 'remained a devout editorialist for Irish land reform ... and for Irish home rule' (Keneally 532).

5. The diary and other evidence indicate that the Cashmans had three children (Catherine actually gave birth to the third on the day Cashman was arrested), but the accounts of their life in Boston mention only William P. Cashman, the eldest of the three. The two younger children, Denis and Arthur, died of measles fourteen months after Cashman's arrest; we do not know whether or not he ever saw his youngest son, his namesake. The 1880 census recorded

a Denis P. Cashmore [*sic*] residing at 3 Beich [*sic*] Glen in Boston (according to city records, 3 Beech Glen was the residence of Denis B. Cashman from 1876 to 1890) with his wife, Kate, a son, William, born in Ireland, and two daughters, Mary and Kathleen, born in the United States.

6. In looking at the city records, I found that there were two Cashmans listed, one spelled Denis and the other Dennis; given the fact that Cashman's name occasionally appears as 'Dennis' among contemporary scholars, the possibility of a misspelling in the city records somewhat clouds the history of his employment in the 1890s. Further, Thomas Keneally reports that when O'Reilly began his last speaking tour, in the winter of 1890, he left *The Pilot* in 'the safe hands of Denis Cashman and [John] Roche' (625), that on the Saturday before his death he 'was back at *The Pilot* office, complaining to Denis Cashman of insomnia' (626), and that Cashman 'at his death was still employed at *The Pilot*' (628).

7. See especially Alexandra Hasluck, *Unwilling Emigrants: A Study of the Convict Period in Western Australia*. There are a number of other convict diaries available. The most popular, John Mitchell's *Jail Journal*, is still in print, but many others — such as John Martin's *Diary on the Mountstuart Elphinstone, Cork to Sydney, 1849*, and John Ward's *Diary Kept on the Norfolk Island, 1841–1842* — exist only in their original manuscript form or, as did Cashman's diary until this publication, in incomplete copies.

8. Patrick O'Farrell estimates that the 'political rebels among the Irish convicts seem relatively few, about 1.5 percent, that is, less that 600 in the entire history of transportation, of whom nearly 500 arrived in the early years of the colony, up to 1806.' He goes on to say that 'social rebels — those convicted of crimes of violent protest against poverty and landlordism — have been estimated at about a fifth' (*The Irish in Australia*, 24).

9. 'In terms of emigration to Australia,' Hassam writes, 'rites of separation may take the form of those wakes held by the Irish for departing members of their community ...; the ceremonial arrival of

Neptune aboard ship to mark the crossing of the equator is a rite of transition; and the welcoming of the emigrants into the houses of family already in Australia by the provision of a communal meal may be seen as a rite of incorporation.' He states further that 'Without rites of separation and incorporation it would be difficult to tell the old from the new; indeed, it is the function of such rites to define that very boundary' (*Sailing to Australia*, 55 & 56). The convicts had no such rites as Hassam describes, and the ones that they had — being marched to the ship in chains, for example — would have been psychologically negative rites whose purpose was not to help them make the transitions but to make each transition more painful. John Boyle O'Reilly's departing ritual, the transfer from Dartmoor to Portland prefatory to boarding the *Hougoumont*, was especially humiliating: 'To give an idea of it, it is enough to say that every article of clothing which a prisoner wears must at once go back to the prison whence he came. It may be an hour, or two, or more, before a single article is drawn from the stores of the receiving prison, — during which time the felon is supremely primitive. To the prison officials this seems highly amusing; but to me, looking at it with the convict's eyes and feelings, the point of the joke was rather obscure' (quoted in Roche, 64).

10. John Sarsfield Casey, who was seasick for much of the voyage, also kept a diary aboard the *Hougoumont*; it begins, as does Cashman's, with the prison routine of 7 October 1867, the day he was informed that he was being sent to Australia. Unlike Cashman, however, he does not comment on this change of fortune, except to express a 'sadness' for those left behind in English prisons (8 October 1867); nor is there any indication that he, like Cashman, began his diary after the journey was already under way (*Journal of a Voyage from Portland to Fremantle on board the Convict Ship 'Hougoumont' Cap Cozens Commander October 12ᵗʰ 1867*, ed. Martin Kevin Cusack, Bryn Mawr, PA, Dorrance & Co, 1988). References to Casey's diary in subsequent notes will be by date.

11. Keneally further suggests that Cashman's organisation of evening song- and story-fests helped O'Reilly. 'Bad weather over,

the Fenians organized their concert parties with Cashman president of the revels. He tried to involve O'Reilly too, without much success at first, but the concert parties operated as a distraction from O'Reilly's perilous scheme [to seize the ship]' (*The Great Shame*, 484). Later, the production of the newspaper, *The Wild Goose*, would provide an additional and even more time-consuming outlet for O'Reilly's energy and talents.

12. In his obituary for John Boyle O'Reilly, Cashman wrote that O'Reilly had developed a plan to seize the ship and, with John Flood as navigator, sail her to America. The plan seems to have been discarded owing to lack of support and to concern over how to manage the two-hundred-plus criminal convicts ('An Obituary,' *Boston Herald*, 24 August 1890).

13. Hassam notes that there were divisions among the emigrants in terms of nationality and of social class, and he argues that nationality — one's 'Englishness' or 'Irishness' — was the more important of the two (*Sailing to Australia*, 130). Appended to Cashman's diary is a description of the convicts as 'the greatest ruffians, the most notorious robbers in England', with whom the Fenians 'did not associate or scarcely speak'. In his account, probably written well after the voyage, Thomas McCarthy Fennell contrasts the Fenians' entertainment to that of the other prisoners, who, he recalls, spent their time telling stories of their previous crimes or planning new crimes to commit in Australia (*Life on a Convict Ship*, 77–79); and John Sarsfield Casey refers to the non-Fenian convicts as 'veterans of crime ... laying plans for the robbery of houses when they again obtain liberty' (24 November 1868). Keith Amos, arguing against the 'brutal ruffian' image of the Fenians 'projected by the conservative loyalists' in Australia, cites (1) the *Hougoumont* captain's report of their behaviour as 'exemplary' and (2) 'the style and manner of the Fenian concert performances, diary entries, journal contributions and religious observances' as creating 'a strong impression that most [Fenians] shared a high-minded consciousness of their Irish culture and a deep commitment to their nation's right to self-determination' (*The Fenians in Australia*, 121).

14. As surprising as it may seem, the *Hougoumont* was not the only convict ship to have a newspaper. Charles Bateson reports that the *Clara* (1864) had *A Voice of our Exiles or the Clara Weekly Journal*, the *Belgravia* (1866) had *The Belgravean Weekly Journal*, and the *Norwood* (1867) had *Norwoodiana or Sayings and Doings on Route to Western Australia* (*The Convict Ships*, 283).

15. John Sarsfield Casey also looked toward Australia with some apprehension, writing that 'it may be some stalwart Irishman now amongst us is doomed to whiten his bones [in] the scorching sand of his land of exile' (2 January 1868). In his entry for 9 January 1868, a day later than Cashman's 'final entry', Casey notes that the 'mainland appears low & sandy the range surmounted by "Bush"', and looks 'in vain for the emerald green hills dotted with sheep'.

16. There is actually a substantial amount of material in the diary after Cashman's formal close on 8 January 1868. He appends a number of poems written by himself and others, many of which appeared in *The Wild Goose*, a mild and brief narrative about their treatment in prison and aboard ship, and the lyrics of a song for his son, Willie. On one page, he gives a brief description of a prisoner picking a gaoler's pocket. Hassam notes that some diarists continue their diaries for a few days (202), but Cashman's additional entries are not dated entries and so I do not consider them part of the diary proper.

Bibliography

Works Cited

Amos, Keith. *The Fenians in Australia: 1865–1880.* Kensington: University of New South Wales Press, 1988.

Bateson, Charles. *The Convict Ships: 1787–1868.* Glasgow: Brown, Son & Ferguson, 1959.

Cashman, Catherine. 'To His Excellency the Lord Lieutenant General and General Governor of Ireland' (13 July 1867): np. National Archives: Dublin.

Cashman, Denis B. *Diary.* East Carolina University Manuscript Archives. 458.1. East Carolina University, Greenville, NC.

'Cashman, Denis.' *Classification List of Fenian Convicts: Fenian Arrests and Discharges: 1866–1869.* Envelope 2, Document II. National Archives: Dublin.

'Cashman, Denis.' *Ireland: Irish Crimes Records: 1862 to 1865.* 104. National Archives: Dublin.

'Death of Denis B. Cashman.' *The Pilot* (16 January 1897): 5.

'Death of a Waterford Patriot.' *The Waterford News* (30 January 1897): 5.

'Denis Cashman.' *Ireland: Irish Crimes Records* I (1866): 155a. National Archives: Dublin.

Evans, A.G. *Fanatic Heart: A Life of John Boyle O'Reilly.* Nedlands: University of Western Australia Press, 1997.

Fennell, Thomas McCarthy. *Life on a Convict Ship or Misery of Penal Exile.* ACC 4458[A]. National Library of Ireland: Dublin.

Fitzpatrick, David. *Oceans of Consolation: Personal Accounts of Irish Migration to Australia.* Ithaca, NY: Cornell University Press, 1994.

Flood, John. *Notebook.* Navan Library, Navan.

Hasluck, Alexandra. 1959. *Unwilling Immigrants: A Study of the Convict Period in Western Australia.* Melbourne: Oxford University Press, 1978.

Hassam, Andrew. *Sailing to Australia: Shipboard diaries by nineteenth-century British emigrants.* Manchester, UK: Manchester University Press, 1994.

Keneally, Thomas. *The Great Shame.* London: Chatto and Windus, 1998.

Madden, Richard R. *The Life and Times of Robert Emmet.* New York: Excelsior Publishing House, 1880.

Newsinger, John. *Fenianism in Mid-Victorian Britain.* Boulder, CO: Pluto, 1994.

'Obituary.' *The Boston Transcript* (11 January 1897): 5.

O'Farrell, Patrick. *The Irish in Australia.* Notre Dame: University of Notre Dame Press, 1987.

O'Farrell, Patrick. *Letters from Irish Australia.* Kensington: University of New South Wales Press, 1984.

O'Reilly, John Boyle. *Moondyne: A Story from the Under-world.* London: Routledge, 1889.

'Papers Pertaining to John Flood.' MS 22,729. National Archives: Dublin.

Roche, James Jeffrey. *Life of John Boyle O'Reilly: Together with His Complete Poems and Speeches.* Philadelphia: John J. McVey, 1891.

Ryan, Daniel, Superintendent. 'Report: Dublin Metropolitan Police' (31 July 1866): np. National Archives: Dublin.

Ryan, George. 'Dennis [*sic*] B. Cashman: Warmly Devoted to His Native Land.' *Bulletin of the Eire Society* 41.5 (1983): np.

'12 January 1867.' *Fenian Police Reports* Carton 4 (1864–1883): np. National Archives, Dublin.

Selected Works Consulted

Amos, Keith. 'John Flood — Fenian Exile.' *The Irish Australians: Selected Articles for Australian and Irish Family Historians.* Society of Australian Genealogists and Ulster Historical Foundation (1984): 38–39.

Erickson, Rica, ed. *The Brand on His Coat: Biographies of Some Western Australian Convicts.* Nedlands, WA: University of Western Australia Press, 1983.

Magilligan, Donald J. 'The Catalpa.' *The Pilot* (October 1987): 39–41.

McGrath, Walter. 'The Fenians in Australia.' *Journal of the Cork Historical and Archeological Society* 93 (1988): 45–54.

McManamin, Francis G. *The American Years of John Boyle O'Reilly.* Washington, DC: The Catholic University of America, 1959.

Moore, Bryce. *The Voyage Out: 100 Years of Sea Travel to Australia.* Fremantle, WA: Fremantle Arts Centre Press, 1991.

Moynihan, John Senan. 'Fenian Prisoners in Western Australia.' *Eire-Ireland* III.2 (Summer 1968): 6–13.

O'Lúing, Seán. *The Fremantle Mission.* Dublin: Anvil Books, 1965.

Pease, Z.W. *The Catalpa Expedition.* New Bedford, MA: George S. Anthony, 1897.

Ryan, George, ed. 'The Australian Connection: Letters Linking Three Concerned Continents.' *Bulletin of the Eire Society* 48.5 (1990): np.